REFLECTIVE LEADERSHIP

365 DAILY AFFIRMATIONS FOR CLARITY, COURAGE, AND CONTRIBUTION

Dan H. Lawrence

BRICKALOW
Publishing House

Denver, Colorado

Published by Brickalow Publishing House
Denver, Colorado

Disclaimer:
This book is for educational and reflective use only. It does not offer legal, financial, or clinical advice. Readers should consult qualified professionals for matters involving leadership, law, finance, or mental health.

Library of Congress Control Number: 2025937431

ISBN (paperback): 979-8-9924153-4-6

ISBN (epub): 979-8-9924153-5-3

Table of Contents

REFLECTIVE LEADERSHIP

365 Daily Affirmations for Clarity, Courage, and Contribution

Introduction

Start Here - Leading with Intention

This isn't a book of leadership tricks or ten-step formulas. It doesn't promise quick influence or instant authority. Instead, it offers something quieter—and more enduring: a daily return to your center.

At its core, this book is a practice. One affirmation. One insight. One reflection question per day. Not to rush through, but to live with. These aren't lessons to master—they're invitations to notice how you lead, and why.

Leadership isn't a checklist. It's how you move through the world. One decision. One conversation. One relationship at a time.

Why Affirmations?

Affirmations, in this book, are not about self-congratulation or hype. They are brief but deliberate reminders of who you are, what you value, and how you choose to show up. When practiced with care, they help bring attention back to what matters. They interrupt the noise. They guide your posture.

In leadership, that re-centering matters. The work is demanding. The pace is relentless. The stakes are often quiet but real. Affirmations offer you a moment to pause—so you can respond with clarity rather than react from urgency.

Who This Book Is For

This is for anyone who leads—with or without a title.

Whether you're managing teams, mentoring others, making hard decisions, or simply trying to show up well in your daily life, these reflections are meant to meet you where you are. You won't find every answer here. What you'll find instead is a steady companion. One that reminds you, especially in difficult moments, of what you already know when you're at your best.

You can use this book alone. Or with a team.

Try one prompt each week in staff meetings. Share a reflection question in a coaching session. Use it in leadership retreats or as part of long-term development. Leadership is relational. These practices work best when they're shared.

The Philosophy Behind the Practice

This book is shaped by values that stretch across traditions: attentiveness, discernment, humility, compassion, and courage. You'll see echoes of Jesuit reflection, Buddhist presence, and servant leadership—but you won't find any of those named directly. The goal isn't to teach from one path, but to draw from the best of many.

What matters is the shape these values take in action:

- Reflection that leads to discernment

- Presence that becomes integrity

- Clarity that makes space for others

- Leadership that is quiet, consistent, and real

You'll notice: this book doesn't emphasize charisma or control. It emphasizes care. The kind that shows up in how you make decisions. In how you hold power. In how you treat people when no one is watching.

How Learning Happens Here

This isn't a book to finish—it's one to return to.

Each day's affirmation, insight, and reflection is brief by design, but not shallow. The learning doesn't come from explanation. It comes from paying attention.

You'll be invited to notice what resonates, where you pause, what draws you back. These aren't leadership lessons to memorize. They're reminders—truths you likely know in your bones but may not name often. The real transformation happens when you begin to act on what you notice.

This book supports that kind of leadership through:

Integration: These pages aren't about adding more to your day. They help you filter what doesn't matter so you can return to what does. When your daily choices line up with your deeper values, your leadership becomes more whole—and more honest.

Discernment: Over time, you'll begin to see the difference between what you're doing out of habit and what you're choosing with intention. That shift—from autopilot to awareness—is where real clarity begins. Discernment is what turns reflection into action.

Unlearning: Some reflections will affirm what you already believe. Others may interrupt your patterns or raise discomfort. Both matter. Growth often begins when you're willing to lay aside what no longer fits.

Practice: Leadership isn't a concept—it's a craft. And like any craft, it strengthens with use. These pages are meant to be lived with, revisited, and absorbed over time—not skimmed once and shelved.

Shared Reflection: Used with a team, these questions can spark honest conversation. One person's insight invites another's. Over time, these shared reflections can shape a culture grounded in purpose, clarity, and trust.

This isn't about becoming someone new. It's about becoming a steadier, more rooted version of the leader you already are. One day at a time. One choice at a time.

How to Use This Book

There's no single right way to move through these pages. What matters is how you let them shape your awareness, your choices, and your presence. Here are a few ways to make the most of the practice:

Daily Use: Begin or end your day with the day's affirmation, insight, and reflection question.

Don't rush. Sit with it. Journal if that helps. Breathe. Let it shift your posture before you move forward.

With a Team: Let these themes shape conversations in meetings or retreats. Share a reflection question. Invite honesty. You don't need a perfect answer—just a place to begin together.

In Leadership Development Spaces: Bring these affirmations into coaching, mentorship, or training sessions. They offer a language for what often goes unnamed—inner clarity, shared purpose, quiet strength.

Whichever path you choose, this book can support you. Not with formulas, but with grounding. Not with performance, but with presence. It's here to help you lead with clarity, reflection, and care—from the inside out.

How This Book Is Structured: A Leadership Arc in Ten Parts

This book isn't meant to be rushed through. It's structured as a journey; a thoughtful, layered progression that follows how leadership tends to develop in real life. Each section builds on the last. Together, they move from inward awareness to outward impact, from early reflection to long-term influence.

You'll begin with the essentials—self-awareness, values, presence—and gradually move into more advanced leadership practices like building systems, mentoring others, and leaving a legacy. The later sections assume you've done the work that came before. That's what makes the arc work: each part prepares you for what's next.

Here's how each section deepens the practice:

1. Leading from Within (40 Days)

Knowing yourself before you lead others.

This section centers leadership in self-awareness. It begins not with doing, but with being. Through daily practice, it nurtures reflection, inner clarity, and personal alignment. These become the root system from which all other aspects of leadership grow.

2. Building Trust and Connection (45 Days)

From self-awareness to relational depth.

With a strong inner foundation, the leader turns outward. This section explores how relational trust emerges from personal integrity. It deepens the capacity to lead through presence, empathy, communication, and care.

3. Facing Challenges with Courage (45 Days)

Meeting difficulty with integrity and discernment.

Once grounded and connected, the leader is ready to meet pressure with purpose. This is where values are tested. The arc supports movement from comfort to conviction, helping leaders remain steady even when tension rises.

Together, these first three parts develop a leader who is rooted internally, attuned relationally, and resilient in the face of challenge.

4. Growing with Feedback and Flexibility (45 Days)

Staying open, flexible, and grounded as you grow.

Leadership evolves through feedback, reflection, and adaptation. This section invites the leader to stay humble and responsive, holding steady in purpose while adjusting the path. Here, leadership becomes dynamic and alive.

5. Focusing on What Matters (40 Days)

Making decisions from a centered place.

Amid constant noise and competing demands, discernment becomes a discipline. This part supports the leader in learning to filter distractions and act with clear, values-aligned intention. It is about depth, not just productivity.

6. Aligning Systems with Purpose (40 Days)

Aligning your environment with your values.

In this section, *systems* mean the structures, routines, and processes that shape how work gets done. These often-unseen elements influence decisions, behavior, and culture. When aligned with your values, they reinforce purpose. When left unexamined, they create drift. This section helps you build systems that support what matters most.

Parts three through six sharpen the leader's ability to grow, to focus on what matters, and to build environments where vision becomes reality.

7. Building Others Up (35 Days)

Growing people, not just outcomes.

Leadership matures when it shifts from holding control to creating capacity. This section is about mentoring, lifting others, and stepping aside with trust. It charts a progression from helping individuals thrive to preparing the next generation of leaders.

8. Leading with Endurance and Balance (35 Days)

Endurance with integrity.

For leadership to last, it must be sustainable. This part focuses on rhythm, rest, and boundaries. It reframes resilience not as grit alone, but as presence that can be renewed. Endurance here is not about striving—it is about wholeness.

9. Leaving a Legacy (39 Days)

Leading today with tomorrow in mind.

This section gathers the threads of all that came before. It shows that legacy is not something left behind at the end, but something shaped moment by moment in how you lead. Through mentorship, modeling, and shared ownership, it points the leader toward impact that endures.

Parts seven through nine move the leader toward generativity. Influence becomes shared. Presence becomes lasting. The focus shifts from control to contribution.

10. The Return (1 Day)

Leadership begins again.

This final page mirrors the beginning. It reinforces that leadership is a loop, not a ladder. After building presence, resilience, systems, and legacy, the leader returns to reflect and begin again—wiser, humbler, and more whole.

One Last Note

This isn't a workbook you complete. It's a companion you return to. A mirror. A map. A pause.

Come back to it when you lose your footing. Return when you need clarity. Begin again, as often as you must.

Leadership doesn't start when you're given authority. It starts when you take responsibility for how you show up.

This path isn't something you complete once and leave behind. It's a rhythm that returns—deeper each time, shaped by presence, tested through experience, and carried forward with care.

You begin with yourself.
You extend care to others.
You withstand pressure with courage.
You grow through change.
You focus your efforts.
You build aligned structures.
You lift others.
You sustain your energy.
You shape what lasts.
Then you return—ready to begin again.

Part 1

Leading from Within

"Knowing yourself before you lead others."

Day 1

I lead from who I am, not just from what I know.

INSIGHT

Expertise matters, but it's your character that builds trust. Leaders who stay connected to their core values make clearer decisions, communicate with more honesty, and earn deeper respect. It's not just what you do. It's who you are when you do it.

REFLECTION QUESTION

This week, how might I choose what I believe is right over what's simply expected?

Day 2

My presence matters more than my perfection.

INSIGHT

You don't have to get everything right. Showing up with honesty, steadiness, and care builds more trust than flawless execution ever will. People remember how you made them feel, not whether you had the perfect plan.

REFLECTION QUESTION

How can I show up today with presence, even if I don't have all the answers?

Day 3

I don't let the urgent get in the way of the important.

INSIGHT

Urgency will always try to take the lead, but what matters most often waits quietly. Lasting impact comes from choosing the important over the immediate.

REFLECTION QUESTION

What truly important work have I put off because urgency keeps winning the day?

Day 4

Accountability starts

with me.

INSIGHT

You can't expect others to own their actions if you don't model it first. When you take responsibility, even for the hard calls, you build credibility. Ownership doesn't weaken your authority; it strengthens your team's respect.

REFLECTION QUESTION

Where do I need to take responsibility before asking it of someone else?

Day 5

I lead better when I make time to think.

INSIGHT

Reflection isn't a luxury, it's a leadership discipline. When you build thinking time into your routine, you make sharper decisions, avoid tunnel vision, and spot patterns before they become problems.

REFLECTION QUESTION

What quiet space am I giving myself to think, plan, and reflect?

Day 6

I build trust through steady, consistent leadership, not charisma.

INSIGHT

Trust isn't earned through charm or performance—it's built through presence, follow-through, and grounded integrity. What you repeat with care matters more than what you say with flair..

REFLECTION QUESTION

What do my daily patterns teach others about how I lead?

Day 7

My actions shape the culture more than my intentions.

INSIGHT

What you do consistently becomes permission for what others do. If you value transparency, model it. If you value kindness, show it. Leadership shapes culture by example, not explanation.

REFLECTION QUESTION

What messages is my behavior sending, whether I intend them or not?

Day 8

I lead from purpose, not from pressure.

INSIGHT

External demands will always be there, but leaders anchored in purpose don't just react, they respond with direction. When your actions reflect what matters most, even difficult days move something forward.

REFLECTION QUESTION

What part of my leadership this week reflects a deeper purpose, not just urgency?

Day 9

Tough calls are part of leadership; I make them with courage

INSIGHT

Leadership requires decisions that won't please everyone. But clarity, fairness, and intentionality help you navigate those moments with integrity. The goal isn't to avoid discomfort, it's to act with conscience.

REFLECTION QUESTION

What decision am I avoiding, and how can I meet it with clarity, care, and courage?

Day 10

I lead with energy that invites trust and calm.

INSIGHT

Leadership is contagious. Whether calm or chaotic, people feel what you bring into the room. Self-awareness and emotional regulation aren't just personal tools; they shape how others show up, too.

REFLECTION QUESTION

What energy do I bring to meetings, and how does it impact the team?

Day 11

I lead with quiet persistence, even when it's hard.

INSIGHT

Progress isn't always loud or visible. It's often the steady decision to keep going—through effort, presence, and care.

REFLECTION QUESTION

Where do I need to show up with quiet persistence this week?

Day 12

*I act with integrity in
the moments that are
unseen.*

INSIGHT

Leadership is tested in quiet decisions. When
your actions reflect your values—without
recognition or reward—you build a reputation
people trust, even in moments of uncertainty.

REFLECTION QUESTION

What private decision have I made recently
that reflects my deepest values?

Day 13

I hold space for reflection, not just reaction.

INSIGHT

Your best insights come in quiet moments, not constant motion. Time to reflect gives you perspective, steadiness, and better judgment. Pausing to reflect isn't a break from leadership, it's a part of it.

REFLECTION QUESTION

What space have I created this week to think more deeply?

Day 14

I name what matters.

INSIGHT

If you don't speak your values, they get lost in the noise. Good leaders name what's important clearly, consistently, and early so their teams know what to align with.

REFLECTION QUESTION

What principle or value do I need to bring into the conversation today?

Day 15

I lead with presence,

not performance.

INSIGHT

Leadership isn't about putting on a show. It's about being real. When you bring your full attention, without posturing or pressure, you create trust and space for others to be real too.

REFLECTION QUESTION

Where might I be trying to impress instead of simply showing up?

Day 16

I lead with humility so I can continue to grow.

INSIGHT

Humility isn't weakness—it's a commitment to keep learning. It invites collaboration, strengthens relationships, and keeps your leadership grounded in curiosity, not certainty.

REFLECTION QUESTION

Where can I practice humility in my decisions or conversations this week?

Day 17

I lead with consistency to build lasting credibility.

INSIGHT

People remember patterns, not promises. When your words and actions align over time, you earn something deeper than authority: you earn belief.

REFLECTION QUESTION

What consistent actions reinforce the kind of leader I want to be?

Day 18

I lead today with the future in mind.

INSIGHT

Big-picture thinking isn't separate from daily action, it's shaped by it. Every task, every choice, every conversation builds momentum toward the future you want to lead.

REFLECTION QUESTION

How is today's work aligned with the future I want to create?

Day 19

I remain steady when others feel uncertain.

INSIGHT

Leadership isn't about knowing everything, it's about showing up grounded. Calm isn't passivity; it's reassurance. Even in the unknown, your steadiness is a source of trust.

REFLECTION QUESTION

Where can I offer a steady presence when the path ahead feels uncertain?

Day 20

I align my reactions with my values.

INSIGHT

Leadership shows up in the in-between moments—how you respond to stress, criticism, or surprise. When your reactions reflect your values, you build trust without saying a word. Alignment isn't about control, it's about being rooted.

REFLECTION QUESTION

How do my reactions reflect the leader I'm becoming?

Day 21

I show courage in my

quiet decisions.

INSIGHT

Big risks get attention, but daily courage is quieter. It's found in the email you send, the boundaries you hold, and the moments you act on principle.

REFLECTION QUESTION

Where have I shown quiet courage lately?

Day 22

I respond with intention, not impulse.

INSIGHT

When emotions run high, thoughtful leaders don't rush. They pause, reflect, and act with purpose. That pause is not weakness, it's wisdom.

REFLECTION QUESTION

Where might a pause lead to a better outcome?

Day 23

I follow through with others to stay true to myself.

INSIGHT

Before follow-through builds trust with others, it builds integrity within. Honoring your commitments, especially the quiet ones, shapes how you see yourself. It's not about perfection. It's about alignment.

REFLECTION QUESTION

What promise or commitment needs my attention today?

Day 24

My example is a quiet force.

INSIGHT

You don't need to lead loudly to lead effectively. Consistent, values-aligned behavior influences more than rules or slogans ever could.

REFLECTION QUESTION

What am I teaching simply by how I behave?

Day 25

I lead by trusting others to grow alongside me.

INSIGHT

Pressure can tempt you to cut corners or abandon what matters. Leadership isn't control, it's shared growth. Trust invites others to rise and deepens humility within you.

REFLECTION QUESTION

What value do I need to protect in this high-pressure moment?

Day 26

I lead from alignment, not approval.

INSIGHT

The need for approval is a heavy burden. Leading from alignment, where your actions match your values, brings freedom, focus, and strength.

REFLECTION QUESTION

Where can I release control to build trust?

Day 27

I honor the boundaries that keep me whole.

INSIGHT

You can't lead well if you lose yourself in the process. Boundaries aren't barriers, they're acts of self-respect. They protect your clarity, energy, and wholeness. Holding them isn't withdrawal, it's how you stay rooted in who you are.

REFLECTION QUESTION

Where this week do I need to hold a boundary to stay true to myself?

Day 28

I stay grounded in values, even under pressure.

INSIGHT

Pressure reveals character. Staying anchored in what matters most—even when speed, stress, or stakes are high—is what makes leadership real.

REFLECTION QUESTION

What value am I practicing when things get tough?

Day 29

I lead by example when it matters most.

INSIGHT

Anyone can model good behavior when it's easy. What you choose to do under pressure is what others will remember, and often, what they will follow.

REFLECTION QUESTION

What example am I setting, especially when it's hard?

Day 30

I stay consistent, even
when it's inconvenient.

INSIGHT

It's easy to act in alignment when things go smoothly. But consistency through difficulty, that's what earns trust, respect, and long-term credibility.

REFLECTION QUESTION

Where am I tempted to cut corners, and what does consistency require?

Day 31

I face tough decisions in a way that reveals my character, not just my strategy.

INSIGHT

Leadership isn't tested when things are simple. It's tested in moments of tension when values meet risk.

REFLECTION QUESTION

What hard decision can I face in a way that reflects who I am, not just what I know?

Day 32

I create stability by being consistent.

INSIGHT

Teams don't need perfection, they need dependability. When your values and actions match, others feel secure.

REFLECTION QUESTION

Where does my consistency offer more than I realize?

Day 33

My integrity outlasts

my title.

INSIGHT

Reputation fades. Roles change. But the way you show up, the alignment between who you say you are and how you behave, sticks.

REFLECTION QUESTION

Where might staying true to my values matter more than being liked or affirmed in my role?

Day 34

I begin with stillness

before I begin to lead.

INSIGHT

In the quiet, you hear your true voice. Before you act, speak, or decide, pause. Stillness isn't inactivity; it's preparation. When your leadership flows from a grounded center, it carries clarity, humility, and strength.

REFLECTION QUESTION

What space can I create today to listen inward before I lead outward?

Day 35

I honor my own worth as the foundation of how I lead.

INSIGHT

Leadership begins with how you see yourself. When you believe in your own dignity, you lead with clearer boundaries, steadier presence, and deeper trust. Self-worth isn't self-centered, it's what keeps you grounded when pressure rises and others look to you for direction.

REFLECTION QUESTION

Where can I lead this week from self-respect instead of self-doubt?

Day 36

*I inspire others most
when I'm grounded in
my own truth.*

INSIGHT

You don't have to be loud to be inspiring, you just have to be aligned. Real conviction invites others to find their own.

REFLECTION QUESTION

What belief or value keeps me grounded?

Day 37

I speak with courage when silence would be safer.

INSIGHT

Avoidance rarely earns respect. Honest, values-aligned dialogue—especially when it's hard—builds lasting trust.

REFLECTION QUESTION

What truth have I been waiting too long to say?

Day 38

I lead first by how I show up.

INSIGHT

Leadership begins in presence. Before you influence outcomes, you influence the moment through your steadiness, your attention, and your values in action. Even when the path is unclear, how you show up becomes the first act of leadership.

REFLECTION QUESTION

Where today can I lead by showing up with steadiness and intention?

Day 39

I lead from stillness, not urgency.

INSIGHT

Stillness isn't just preparation, it's how real leadership moves through the world. When you lead from a steady center, you create space for clarity, compassion, and wiser choices. True presence isn't rushed. It's rooted.

REFLECTION QUESTION

What practice helps me return to stillness before I act?

Day 40

I lead others best when I stay true to myself.

INSIGHT

Leadership that lasts begins with alignment. When you stay rooted in your values and centered in your presence, you create space for others to grow, contribute, and trust themselves. Your example invites others to lead, not by control, but by clarity.

REFLECTION QUESTION

How does staying rooted in who I am shape the trust I build with others?

Part 2

Building Trust and Connection

"From self-awareness to relational depth."

Day 41

Listening is not passive, it's powerful.

INSIGHT

People don't need you to solve everything. They need to know they've been heard. Listening, without immediately fixing or defending, builds psychological safety and stronger teams. It's one of the most strategic things you can do.

REFLECTION QUESTION

How can I make space today to really listen, especially when I feel rushed?

Day 42

I hold both accountability and compassion.

INSIGHT

Being direct and being kind aren't opposites. Clear expectations and human-centered leadership can, and should, coexist. It's possible to challenge someone while still honoring their dignity.

REFLECTION QUESTION

How can I address a challenge directly while staying grounded in respect?

Day 43

I lead with empathy by seeking to understand, not just agree.

INSIGHT

You don't have to agree to respect someone's experience. Empathy bridges perspectives, especially in conflict, by turning tension into connection through the simple act of seeing one another.

REFLECTION QUESTION

Where could empathy open a stuck conversation or strained relationship?

Day 44

I pause before I respond, especially when emotions are high.

INSIGHT

Emotional discipline isn't about bottling things up, it's about creating space between reaction and response. In that space, leadership chooses intention over impulse.

REFLECTION QUESTION

Where can a moment of pause give me better clarity this week?

Day 45

I create shared clarity so our goals stay focused and meaningful..

INSIGHT

When people know where they're going—and why—they engage with more energy and trust. Clear, visible goals aligned with shared purpose build both direction and commitment.

REFLECTION QUESTION

How can I help the team connect to and take ownership of our shared goals?

Day 46

I confront conflict with clarity and care.

INSIGHT

Avoiding conflict doesn't preserve peace—it delays progress. Addressing it early, honestly, and respectfully prevents small issues from becoming cultural cracks. Clarity means naming the real issue. Care means respecting the person, even while facing the problem. Conflict isn't the problem—how we handle it is.

REFLECTION QUESTION

What's one hard conversation I've been avoiding, and how can I lead into it?

Day 47

I don't carry everything alone.

INSIGHT

Strong leadership isn't about bearing every burden, it's about building systems and relationships that can share the load. Trusting others isn't a sign of weakness; it's how resilience is sustained.

REFLECTION QUESTION

What can I delegate or share this week to lead more sustainably?

Day 48

I offer steadiness and direction in uncertain times.

INSIGHT

You don't need all the answers to lead through uncertainty. Steadiness reassures; direction provides hope. When you stay grounded and offer a clear next step, you help others find their footing—even when the full path isn't yet clear..

REFLECTION QUESTION

How can I offer steadiness and a next step when things feel uncertain?

Day 49

I lead by lifting others.

INSIGHT

Recognition, encouragement, opportunity. Small acts of support build strong teams. Leadership isn't just about direction; it's about elevation.

REFLECTION QUESTION

Who could use a reminder today that their work matters?

Day 50

I create momentum through small wins.

INSIGHT

Progress doesn't always start with breakthroughs. It starts with follow-ups, clean handoffs, and small, visible progress. Celebrating what's working keeps the energy moving forward.

REFLECTION QUESTION

What's one small win I can name and build on this week?

Day 51

I make space for voices that aren't always heard.

INSIGHT

Powerful leadership isn't about always speaking, it's about knowing when to listen. Making space for quieter voices or underrepresented perspectives creates stronger, more inclusive decisions.

REFLECTION QUESTION

Who hasn't spoken yet, and how can I invite them in?

Day 52

I honor trust by speaking the truth with care.

INSIGHT

Honesty is not just about bravery, it's about respect. When you speak the truth with care, you build the kind of trust that endures. Silence might feel safer in the moment, but truth strengthens connection over time.

REFLECTION QUESTION

What truth, if spoken with care, could build trust today?

Day 53

I approach conflict as
a chance to build trust.

INSIGHT

Handled well, conflict is clarifying. It shows
where expectations differ, values surface, and
relationships grow. Avoiding it robs teams of
the chance to become stronger.

REFLECTION QUESTION

What tension could become trust if I stepped
into it with care?

Day 54

I speak with purpose,

not just volume.

INSIGHT

Influence doesn't require a loud voice, just a clear one. When your words are thoughtful and aligned with your values, people listen.

REFLECTION QUESTION

Am I using my voice to contribute or to fill space?

Day 55

I learn from those I lead.

INSIGHT

Leadership is reciprocal. Staying open to learning from your team, whether through feedback, mistakes, or observation, keeps you humble and evolving.

REFLECTION QUESTION

What has my team taught me lately?

Day 56

I ask better questions
instead of rushing to
fix.

INSIGHT

Not every problem needs a fast solution. Sometimes, it needs space to unfold. Questions open possibility, answers close it. Leadership lives in curiosity.

REFLECTION QUESTION

Where could a better question serve more than a quick solution?

Day 57

I am not the only source of good ideas.

INSIGHT

Leaders don't need to have all the answers, they need to create space for answers to emerge. Invite others in, and you'll lead with more insight and less ego.

REFLECTION QUESTION

Whose voice haven't I considered?

Day 58

I create psychological safety by how I show up.

INSIGHT

How you respond to feedback, questions, or failure either invites openness or shuts it down. Trust grows where people feel safe to speak, take risks, and grow.

REFLECTION QUESTION

What do my reactions teach others about what's safe here?

Day 59

I notice what others overlook.

INSIGHT

Strong leaders pay attention, not just to outcomes, but to people, energy, effort, and change. Recognition begins with observation.

REFLECTION QUESTION

Who or what have I overlooked lately?

Day 60

I lead better when I stay curious.

INSIGHT

Assumptions close doors. Curiosity opens them. Leaders who stay curious ask better questions, uncover better answers, and build better relationships.

REFLECTION QUESTION

Where could curiosity help more than certainty?

Day 61

Listening is my first leadership move.

INSIGHT

Leadership begins by creating space, not by taking charge. Listening signals that others' voices matter—and when people feel heard, trust and clarity grow. Often, the best solutions emerge when you start by simply making room.

REFLECTION QUESTION

Where can creating space through listening lead to stronger trust today?

Day 62

I listen fully, because understanding builds trust.

INSIGHT

When people feel heard, they open up. Listening with full attention creates psychological safety and invites honesty.

REFLECTION QUESTION

How can I show someone I've truly heard them today?

Day 63

Trust is built in the quiet follow-through.

INSIGHT

You don't need grand gestures to build credibility, just consistency. Teams trust leaders who do what they say, even when no one's watching.

REFLECTION QUESTION

What's one small commitment I need to keep today?

Day 64

I stay curious, even when I think I know.

INSIGHT

Curiosity keeps leadership fresh. It helps you see what others miss, adapt when things shift, and avoid the trap of assumption.

REFLECTION QUESTION

Where could curiosity uncover something I've overlooked?

Day 65

I remember that people are greater than processes.

INSIGHT

Systems keep things running, but relationships give them meaning. Leadership grounded in empathy—not just efficiency—builds trust that lasts.

REFLECTION QUESTION

Where might I be prioritizing process over people?

Day 66

I stay connected through disagreement, with respect and purpose.

INSIGHT

Shared purpose doesn't require full agreement. When grounded in curiosity and respect, connection can deepen even in tension—and disagreement can lead to better outcomes than consensus alone.

REFLECTION QUESTION

Where can I stay connected, even if I disagree?

Day 67

The best ideas often come from listening, not leading.

INSIGHT

If you're always talking, you're not learning. Listening creates space for innovation, inclusion, and understanding. All essential ingredients for progress.

REFLECTION QUESTION

When was the last time I listened without preparing a response?

Day 68

I ask questions to uncover meaning, not just to get answers.

INSIGHT

Leadership is less about giving direction and more about making space for discovery. The right questions reveal hidden needs, values, and possibilities that might otherwise go unnoticed.

REFLECTION QUESTION

What question could help me understand more than I assume?

Day 69

I nurture trust by listening, not solving.

INSIGHT

People don't always need answers, they need attention. When you listen without rushing to fix, you earn trust that lasts.

REFLECTION QUESTION

Where can I slow down and simply listen?

Day 70

I don't just lead tasks, I support people.

INSIGHT

It's easy to get caught in the grind. But real leadership is relational. Pay attention to the people, not just the performance.

REFLECTION QUESTION

Who might need support from me beyond the checklist?

Day 71

I grow by asking, not assuming.

INSIGHT

Leadership isn't about having all the answers. It's about staying open, especially to what others can teach you. Humility invites trust, and trust keeps teams strong. Curiosity keeps you learning, and learning keeps you leading.

REFLECTION QUESTION

Where could asking, rather than assuming, open a door I didn't expect?

Day 72

I lead better when I see others fully.

INSIGHT

Recognition isn't about ego, it's about connection. See the effort. Acknowledge the person. Leadership becomes human through attention.

REFLECTION QUESTION

Who deserves to be seen for more than just their results?

Day 73

I lead with clarity that builds confidence, not fear.

INSIGHT

Clarity empowers people to act with purpose. When teams know what matters, they can take initiative. When clarity fades, people shrink. Make things plain, and watch people grow.

REFLECTION QUESTION

What part of my vision needs to be said out loud?

Day 74

I lead with silence
when presence speaks
loudest.

INSIGHT

You don't have to fill every space. Often, stillness lets others find their own clarity. Presence doesn't always need words.

REFLECTION QUESTION

Where might silence invite something valuable?

Day 75

I nurture the relationships that empower my growth.

INSIGHT

Leadership flourishes when it's supported by trust, openness, and genuine connection. Investing in people is an investment in your own evolution.

REFLECTION QUESTION

Who in my circle would benefit from deeper engagement today?

Day 76

I honor the uniqueness of every perspective I encounter.

INSIGHT

Diverse viewpoints enrich leadership. Valuing each voice not only broadens your vision but deepens the collective wisdom.

REFLECTION QUESTION

What new perspective have I encountered today that I can learn from?

Day 77

I speak my truth with precision and care.

INSIGHT

Clear, honest communication lays the groundwork for strong relationships.

REFLECTION QUESTION

What conversation can I refine with greater clarity today?

Day 78

I lead by listening deeply and responding with empathy.

INSIGHT

The act of listening transforms dialogues into collaborative discoveries.

REFLECTION QUESTION

How can my active listening empower someone today?

Day 79

*I clarify expectations
with kindness and
firmness, guiding
others toward success.*

INSIGHT

Clear communication is both an art and a discipline. It builds trust and sets the stage for achievement.

REFLECTION QUESTION

What goal or process could benefit from a clearer, kinder explanation today?

Day 80

*I lead by connecting
authentically with
those around me.*

INSIGHT

When I take time to build genuine relationships, I create a network of support that underpins all my successes.

REFLECTION QUESTION

Who in my circle could benefit from a more authentic connection today?

Day 81

I value diverse viewpoints to enhance my vision.

INSIGHT

Welcoming a range of perspectives enriches my decision-making and strengthens my leadership.

REFLECTION QUESTION

What new perspective have I encountered that challenges my assumptions?

Day 82

I encourage others in ways that outlast the moment.

INSIGHT

Encouragement isn't just a quick boost, it's an investment in someone's belief about themselves. When you see someone's effort and name their potential, you plant confidence that can shape their future.

REFLECTION QUESTION

Who could benefit from being reminded of their strength today?

Day 83

I notice and name the contributions others might miss.

INSIGHT

Not all great work comes with a headline. Behind-the-scenes effort and steady consistency often go unseen unless we choose to honor it. Recognition strengthens culture and connection.

REFLECTION QUESTION

Who is making an impact behind the scenes, and how can I acknowledge them?

Day 84

I move forward with grace, not force.

INSIGHT

Leadership is not about pushing harder, it's about moving intentionally. Grace brings others with you. Force leaves them behind.

REFLECTION QUESTION

What would leading with grace look like today?

Day 85

I offer clarity as an act of care.

INSIGHT

Avoiding hard conversations may feel kind in the moment, but it creates confusion and distance. Clarity, delivered with humility and presence, respects the dignity of all involved.

REFLECTION QUESTION

Where could clear, compassionate truth deepen trust today?

Part 3

Facing Challenges with Courage

"Meeting difficulty with integrity and discernment."

Day 86

I don't need all the answers to lead well.

INSIGHT

Good leaders ask strong questions. Trying to have every solution can shut down collaboration and limit growth. Admitting what you don't know isn't a weakness, it's an invitation to build trust, learn, and lead with others.

REFLECTION QUESTION

Where could I model curiosity over certainty this week?

Day 87

I slow down when the pressure speeds up.

INSIGHT

Urgency makes it tempting to rush decisions—but that's when mistakes happen. Pausing doesn't mean indecision. It's how strong leaders create space for discernment, strategy, and better outcomes.

REFLECTION QUESTION

Where might a pause improve the quality of my next decision?

Day 88

I can give a clear "no" and be more powerful than when giving a hesitant "yes."

INSIGHT

Boundaries protect your focus and your integrity. Saying no isn't selfish, it's strategic. When you say yes to everything, you dilute your effectiveness.

REFLECTION QUESTION

Where do I need to say no, so I can lead with more focus?

Day 89

I invite challenge, not just agreement.

INSIGHT

Dissent is not disloyalty. Welcoming pushback shows that you value truth over comfort. A culture of curiosity starts with a leader willing to be questioned.

REFLECTION QUESTION

How do I respond when someone disagrees with me?

I don't lead to be liked,
I lead to make a
difference.

INSIGHT

If popularity becomes your compass, you'll lose direction. Leaders who lead with conviction won't always be liked, but they will be remembered for doing what mattered.

REFLECTION QUESTION

Where am I prioritizing comfort over impact?

Day 91

I choose courage over comfort when it matters most.

INSIGHT

Leadership will ask more of you than you're ready to give. Growth doesn't come from what's easy, it comes from what's right, especially when it's hard.

REFLECTION QUESTION

Where am I being invited to act courageously?

Day 92

I honor the process, not just the result.

INSIGHT

Results matter. But how you get there matters more. When you value the journey—how you treat people, how you make decisions—you create outcomes worth following.

REFLECTION QUESTION

What part of the process deserves more attention right now?

Day 93

I show courage by living my values, even when it's uncomfortable.

INSIGHT

It's easy to act on your values when it's convenient. Real leadership shows when you stay true under pressure—building trust through courageous action.

REFLECTION QUESTION

Where might showing up with integrity feel uncomfortable, but necessary, this week?

Day 94

I lean into tension with honesty and curiosity, knowing it can lead to transformation..

INSIGHT

Conflict isn't the enemy—avoidance is. When met with openness, the tension of conflict becomes a source of clarity, connection, and change. Step into it with honesty and curiosity.

REFLECTION QUESTION

What tension could be useful if I leaned into it?

Day 95

I don't fear hard conversations; I prepare for them.

INSIGHT

Preparation builds courage. When you enter a tough conversation with care and clarity, you open the door to growth.

REFLECTION QUESTION

What difficult conversation deserves more preparation than avoidance?

Day 96

I strengthen relationships through courageous conversations.

INSIGHT

Avoidance erodes trust. Honest dialogue, even when it is uncomfortable, fosters deeper connections, respect, and collaboration.

REFLECTION QUESTION

What conversation am I avoiding, and how might it help, not hurt?

Day 97

*I lead with courage
and care in every
conversation.*

INSIGHT

Tough conversations don't have to be harsh. They can be honest and human. That tone creates teams that can grow together.

REFLECTION QUESTION

How can I bring care into a conversation that needs courage?

Day 98

I build bridges through honest, humble dialogue.

INSIGHT

It's rarely the topic that breaks trust—it's the tone. When truth is delivered with care and humility, even hard conversations can deepen connection.

REFLECTION QUESTION

What relationship could grow through honest conversation?

Day 99

I resolve conflict by aligning values, not by avoiding discomfort.

INSIGHT

Avoidance creates distance. Real resolution happens when we name our values and work toward alignment, not agreement.

REFLECTION QUESTION

What honest conversation could move a situation forward?

Day 100

I choose what's right,

not what's easy.

INSIGHT

The temptation to sidestep ethics is rarely dramatic—it's subtle. It shows up in shortcuts, silence, or "just this once." Stay aligned.

REFLECTION QUESTION

What decision today could either build or erode my credibility?

Day 101

I choose what's right,

even when it's

unpopular..

INSIGHT

Leadership grounded in integrity doesn't chase approval. Upholding truth or boundaries may disappoint some, but it protects what matters most.

REFLECTION QUESTION

What principle am I protecting, even when it's hard?

Day 102

I lead from values,
even when results are
uncertain.

INSIGHT

Outcomes shift. Metrics change. But values hold. If your foundation is steady, your direction stays true—even when the road bends.

REFLECTION QUESTION

What value am I refusing to trade for convenience?

Day 103

Even when no one is watching—I still lead.

INSIGHT

Integrity is internal. It's not performance—it's commitment. What you do when it's hard or hidden shows who you are.

REFLECTION QUESTION

What private action today reflects my deepest values?

Day 104

I lead systems that reflect my values.

INSIGHT

Your personal integrity can't make up for broken processes. Leadership includes shaping systems that support equity, well-being, and purpose.

REFLECTION QUESTION

What system in my life or work could better reflect my values?

Day 105

I take responsibility
for what I shape—even
unintentionally.

INSIGHT

Leaders influence culture with every action. Even habits and unspoken norms grow from the behaviors you tolerate or model.

REFLECTION QUESTION

What culture am I reinforcing—on purpose or by accident?

Day 106

I am responsible for my ripple effect.

INSIGHT

What you normalize, encourage, or ignore sets the tone for others. Awareness of your influence is a mark of maturity.

REFLECTION QUESTION

Where might I be shaping more than I realize?

Day 107

I challenge systems
that no longer serve.

INSIGHT

Not all inherited structures deserve to stay.
Part of leadership is the courage to reimagine
what's possible.

REFLECTION QUESTION

What structure am I accepting that needs to be
redesigned?

Day 108

I hold others

accountable with care.

INSIGHT

Accountability doesn't have to be harsh. When it's grounded in shared purpose and respect, it becomes an act of service—not discipline.

REFLECTION QUESTION

Where can I hold someone accountable without shame?

Day 109

I dare to experiment
even when the outcome
is uncertain.

INSIGHT

Every risk taken with intention is an opportunity to learn and evolve.

REFLECTION QUESTION

What small risk can I take today that might open up new possibilities?

Day 110

I allow my actions to speak louder than my words.

INSIGHT

By acting consistently with your values, you leave a silent but powerful message for others to follow.

REFLECTION QUESTION

In what recent moment did my actions define my leadership?

Day 111

I engage in courageous conversations that build bridges, not walls.

INSIGHT

Accountability isn't about blame—it's about honoring shared purpose with respect. When done well, it becomes an act of service, not discipline.

REFLECTION QUESTION

What difficult conversation can I approach with openness today?

Day 112

I stay steady under
pressure, finding
strength in
vulnerability.

INSIGHT

Vulnerability in leadership isn't a weakness—
it's the courage to be genuine.

REFLECTION QUESTION

Where can I safely share my uncertainties to
foster genuine connection?

Day 113

I embrace challenges

as opportunities to

lead with resolve.

INSIGHT

Difficult moments are invitations to demonstrate not only competence but also care and courage.

REFLECTION QUESTION

When was the last time I led with both strength and care in a difficult moment—and what did it reveal about my leadership?

Day 114

*I align my daily
practices with my
deepest values.*

INSIGHT

My daily routines are a reflection of my inner
priorities; aligning them ensures that my
actions are true to who I am and who I strive to
be.

REFLECTION QUESTION

In what way do my current practices mirror my
core values?

Day 115

I cultivate open dialogue that respects and unites us.

INSIGHT

When conversations are honest and inclusive, barriers break down and ideas flourish.

REFLECTION QUESTION

How can I encourage a more open exchange of ideas today?

Day 116

I balance my vision with compassion in every decision.

INSIGHT

Strong leadership unites strategic insight with genuine care for people's well-being.

REFLECTION QUESTION

How can I infuse empathy into my strategic choices today?

Day 117

I lead with conviction, blending vision with genuine care.

INSIGHT

When my decisions honor both my strategic goals and the humanity around me, my leadership resonates deeply.

REFLECTION QUESTION

In what way can I better balance my vision with empathy today?

Day 118

Decisive action is strongest when rooted in discernment

INSIGHT

Leadership grows when decisions are guided by thoughtful reflection—not just speed. In moments of ambiguity, it's not clarity alone that leads—it's the courage to act with inner alignment.

REFLECTION QUESTION

How can I lead with both reflection and resolve today?

Day 119

I open myself to candid

conversations about

my challenges.

INSIGHT

Sharing your struggles can illuminate new paths and foster deeper trust.

REFLECTION QUESTION

Who can I invite into a genuine dialogue about an ongoing challenge?

Day 120

*My inner resolve
guides me through
external challenges.*

INSIGHT

When obstacles arise, my inner strength gives me clear direction, independent of others' opinions.

REFLECTION QUESTION

Which internal resource can I call upon to overcome a current challenge?

Day 121

I transform challenges into opportunities that uplift others.

INSIGHT

Every difficulty presents a chance to demonstrate resilience and foster collective progress through honest dialogue.

REFLECTION QUESTION

How can a current challenge serve as an opportunity for community growth?

Day 122

I lead by serving with authenticity and deep commitment.

INSIGHT

My leadership is not measured by the accolades I receive but by the trust and growth I cultivate in others.

REFLECTION QUESTION

In what concrete way can I serve my community today?

Day 123

I lead not for fleeting accolades, but to spark lasting, meaningful change.

INSIGHT

When my leadership is rooted in purpose and authenticity, the impact I create endures beyond momentary praise.

REFLECTION QUESTION

What decision today contributes to the transformative change I envision?

Day 124

I lead for the long haul, not the headlines.

INSIGHT

Recognition fades. Impact endures. Keep showing up with care, consistency, and clarity—and the work will speak for itself.

REFLECTION QUESTION

What long-term impact am I committed to, even without praise?

Day 125

I lead like someone else will inherit this.

INSIGHT

Treat today's systems, teams, and cultures as if someone you care about will step into your shoes. Because one day, they will.

REFLECTION QUESTION

What kind of environment am I shaping for the people who come next?

Day 126

I treat each decision as part of something larger.

INSIGHT

Today's choices ripple outward. Even the smallest act can carry purpose when it aligns with something bigger.

REFLECTION QUESTION

How does this decision support what I want to leave behind?

Day 127

My legacy is shaped by the values I protect.

INSIGHT

It's not always your title or your achievements that endure. It's how clearly you lived your values when it mattered most.

REFLECTION QUESTION

What value do I want people to remember me for—and am I honoring it today?

Day 128

I taker the long view to make today's effort meaningful.

INSIGHT

When you lift your eyes beyond the task, you remember what you're really building. Perspective makes even the hard days part of something lasting.

REFLECTION QUESTION

What future am I helping to shape through today's choices?

What I model is what I multiply.

INSIGHT

You teach more by example than by explanation. If you want your legacy to include compassion, clarity, or courage, show it now.

REFLECTION QUESTION

What lesson is my leadership teaching today?

Day 130

*My leadership carries
a thread of continuity
across generations.*

INSIGHT

You are part of something bigger—shaped by
those before you, shaping those who follow.
Lead as if your voice echoes in future rooms.

REFLECTION QUESTION

What legacy am I continuing—and what legacy
am I creating?

Part 4

Growing with Feedback and Flexibility

"Staying open, flexible, and grounded as you grow."

Day 131

I lean into discomfort as a path to growth..

INSIGHT

Comfort zones protect us, but they rarely stretch us. Leadership requires discomfort, trying new approaches, owning mistakes, facing resistance. That tension is where learning happens.

REFLECTION QUESTION

Where am I being invited to stretch right now?

Day 132

I welcome feedback as
a pathway to growth.

INSIGHT

Feedback can sting, but it's also the doorway to better outcomes, better leadership, and better relationships. Growth-minded leaders learn to welcome input and separate their identity from their performance.

REFLECTION QUESTION

How can I make feedback less threatening, and more valuable, for myself or my team?

Day 133

I create space to absorb, reflect, and adjust.

INSIGHT

Growth isn't just about reacting quickly, it's about creating space to process, reflect, and integrate. True flexibility requires time to let insights settle before shaping the next move.

REFLECTION QUESTION

Where am I ignoring rest, and what is it costing me and others?

Day 134

I lead with adaptability, not rigidity.

INSIGHT

Being willing to shift doesn't mean abandoning your principles. It means staying responsive to what's real. Rigidity breaks under pressure; adaptability bends and builds momentum in a new direction.

REFLECTION QUESTION

Where am I resisting change that might actually serve the mission?

Day 135

Every challenge is an invitation to grow.

INSIGHT

Not every problem is a failure. Some are opportunities in disguise—testing your patience, creativity, or humility. Growth doesn't always come from wins. Often, it's what you learn in the hard stretch that builds your capacity.

REFLECTION QUESTION

What's one challenge I'm facing—and what is it asking me to learn?

Day 136

I use feedback to sharpen my growth.

INSIGHT

Feedback isn't just about correction—it's about direction. Every critique can help sharpen your insight, strengthen your leadership, and build resilience—if you're open enough to listen.

REFLECTION QUESTION

What recent feedback am I resisting—and what can I learn from it?

Day 137

I learn from mistakes

without losing myself.

INSIGHT

You are not your last failure. Mistakes are part of the feedback loop that leads to better decisions. What matters is how you respond— how you repair, adjust, and continue to grow.

REFLECTION QUESTION

What mistake am I ready to stop carrying—and start learning from?

Day 138

I stay open to new ways forward.

INSIGHT

Adaptability doesn't mean abandoning the goal, it means rethinking the path. When you let go of rigid thinking, you open the door to innovation and progress.

REFLECTION QUESTION

Where might a new approach serve the outcome better than the old plan?

Day 139

I grow by making time to reflect.

INSIGHT

Growth isn't only measured in output. It's measured in awareness. Taking time to reflect gives your leadership depth and helps prevent repeated mistakes.

REFLECTION QUESTION

What lesson have I learned recently that I haven't yet applied?

Day 140

I build clarity into every conversation.

INSIGHT

Confusion is costly. Clear expectations, consistent communication, and honest follow-up build trust. Don't assume people understand—make sure they do.

REFLECTION QUESTION

What conversation needs more clarity from me?

Day 141

I am patient with the

process of change.

INSIGHT

Transformation doesn't always move fast, but it does move. Real change requires patience, consistency, and a willingness to walk through discomfort.

REFLECTION QUESTION

What process am I trying to rush—and what would patience look like?

Day 142

I trust that adaptability strengthens me—it doesn't diminish me.

INSIGHT

Plans change. Leaders evolve. Flexibility shows you're learning. It's not indecision—it's strategic adjustment.

REFLECTION QUESTION

What outdated approach do I need to release?

Day 143

I recognize discomfort as a possible sign of growth.

INSIGHT

Change is rarely comfortable, but that doesn't mean it's wrong. Learn to distinguish fear from growth, resistance from readiness.

REFLECTION QUESTION

What discomfort might actually be growth in disguise?

Day 144

I learn from every outcome, even the difficult ones.

INSIGHT

Success teaches. Failure teaches more. Reflection turns experience into wisdom, and wisdom into better leadership next time.

REFLECTION QUESTION

What lesson from a recent outcome could shape my next decision?

Day 145

I keep showing up,
especially when it's
hard.

INSIGHT

Persistence isn't flashy. It's not always recognized. But it's how real progress happens—one honest effort at a time, even when no one sees.

REFLECTION QUESTION

What's one thing I'll keep showing up for, even when it's hard?

Day 146

*I lead with patience
that creates space for
lasting growth.*

INSIGHT

Impatience can erode relationships, derail progress, or burn you out. When you lead with patience, you create room for growth to happen on its own terms.

REFLECTION QUESTION

Where could I practice patience without losing momentum?

Day 147

I honor the quiet progress that keeps me moving forward.

INSIGHT

Leadership grows not in grand gestures, but in steady, unseen work that aligns with your deeper purpose. Quiet effort builds lasting momentum.

REFLECTION QUESTION

What progress am I making that I haven't honored?

Day 148

I recognize the difference between growing tension and draining stress.

INSIGHT

Tension that stretches you toward your purpose is healthy. Stress that pulls you away from your center is not. Knowing the difference protects your growth.

REFLECTION QUESTION

Is the tension I'm feeling helping me stretch—or pulling me off course?

Day 149

I stay open when challenge invites growth.

INSIGHT

Disagreement can be a catalyst for better thinking. Listening deeply in moments of friction transforms tension into new possibility.

REFLECTION QUESTION

Where is disagreement inviting me to learn?

Day 150

I grow by offering feedback as a shared path to learning, not judgment.

INSIGHT

When feedback is about improving the work, not judging the person, it becomes a shared resource for growth, not a wedge for resentment.

REFLECTION QUESTION

How can I offer feedback in a way that supports growth—for them and for me?

Day 151

I lead more wisely when I take time to reflect..

INSIGHT

Leadership moves fast—but wisdom takes pause. Reflection isn't a break from leading; it's how you stay aligned, intentional, and steady when it matters most.

REFLECTION QUESTION

Where in my leadership do I need space to realign before moving forward?

Day 152

I lead with a self-awareness that keeps me grounded.

INSIGHT

Without reflection, ego takes the wheel. Self-awareness helps you lead from your values, not your impulses.

REFLECTION QUESTION

What patterns do I notice in myself that deserve more attention?

Day 153

I create space for feedback to be safe and shared.

INSIGHT

Feedback shouldn't only flow one way. Inviting it—modeling openness—builds a culture where growth is expected, not feared.

REFLECTION QUESTION

When's the last time I asked for feedback—and really listened?

Day 154

I stay open to learning,
even when it
challenges me.

INSIGHT

Growth often arrives disguised as discomfort. When you resist the urge to retreat and instead stay curious, you create space for deeper learning and lasting change.

REFLECTION QUESTION

Where am I being challenged—and what might it be teaching me?

Day 155

I welcome feedback as a gift, even when it stings.

INSIGHT

You don't have to enjoy it to benefit from it. Feedback may be difficult to hear, but it often opens the door to meaningful growth..

REFLECTION QUESTION

What feedback am I avoiding—and what might it reveal?

Day 156

I model growth by embracing my own learning journey.

INSIGHT

When leaders openly engage in their own growth, it encourages others to do the same. Effective leadership is about setting the tone for continuous learning, rather than perfection.

REFLECTION QUESTION

Where can my commitment to growth inspire others?

Day 157

I receive feedback as a mirror, not a verdict.

INSIGHT

Feedback doesn't define you—it reflects what others experience. Let it inform, not diminish you.

REFLECTION QUESTION

What truth might this feedback reveal about how I lead?

Day 158

I model what I want repeated.

INSIGHT

What you repeat becomes culture. Don't just say what matters—live it, reinforce it, and reflect it back.

REFLECTION QUESTION

What pattern am I reinforcing in my team—intentionally or not?

Day 159

I pause to review all I have learned so far.

INSIGHT

Reflection isn't a retreat—it's the starting point for renewed growth. By looking back, you clarify what matters most in your leadership journey.

REFLECTION QUESTION

What key lessons from my past days do I need to carry forward?

Day 160

I embrace both my progress and my setbacks as teachers.

INSIGHT

Every success and every stumble builds the foundation of wisdom. Both are essential for genuine growth.

REFLECTION QUESTION

Which experience recently taught me the most, and why?

Day 161

*I integrate feedback
from my inner voice
and from others.*

INSIGHT

Feedback—whether internal or external—is a guide, not a verdict. When balanced with self-trust, it creates a pathway for steady improvement.

REFLECTION QUESTION

How can I weave recent insights into my daily habits?

Day 162

I balance optimism with realistic appraisal of my journey.

INSIGHT

A grounded view of progress honors both your wins and your areas for growth. Balance keeps your ambition healthy and sustainable.

REFLECTION QUESTION

Where might I be overly optimistic or overly critical in evaluating my progress?

Day 163

*I inspire by sharing
my journey openly.*

INSIGHT

Transparent storytelling fosters trust and encourages others to find their own voice. When you lead with vulnerability, inspiration follows naturally.

REFLECTION QUESTION

What part of my story could inspire someone else right now?

Day 164

I foster collaboration to drive meaningful change.

INSIGHT

When leaders invite diverse perspectives and shared ownership, collaboration becomes a catalyst for innovation and collective growth..

REFLECTION QUESTION

How can I intentionally create space for collaborative input to enhance our current initiatives?

Day 165

I welcome change as a chance to create better solutions.

INSIGHT

Change is not just something to manage, it's raw material for innovation. Leaders who embrace it reshape what's possible.

REFLECTION QUESTION

What change could I actively use to design something stronger?

Day 166

I treat failures as prototypes for better ideas.

INSIGHT

Missteps aren't dead ends, they're blueprints. Every lesson from failure sketches a better, stronger way forward.

REFLECTION QUESTION

What recent stumble is guiding me toward a smarter next step?

Day 167

I strengthen the future through small, steady improvement.

INSIGHT

Sustainable change is rarely sudden; it's crafted through deliberate, consistent upgrades that compound into a transformation.

REFLECTION QUESTION

What is one incremental change I can commit to that will have a ripple effect?

Day 168

I refine my focus to align with evolving purpose.

INSIGHT

Shifting priorities is not failure, it's wisdom. As you grow, refining your focus keeps you aligned with what matters mos.

REFLECTION QUESTION

What priority needs to shift to better reflect today's realities?

Day 169

I honor my journey by learning from every experience.

INSIGHT

The path of leadership is continuously evolving. Embracing both wins and missteps cultivates a deeper understanding of who you are and what you stand for.

REFLECTION QUESTION

How has my journey transformed me, and what do I still need to learn?

Day 170

I embrace challenges
as opportunities for
inner growth.

INSIGHT

Every obstacle is a chance to refine your character and deepen your resilience.

REFLECTION QUESTION

What recent challenge has strengthened my resolve?

Day 171

I invite rigorous feedback to refine my approach.

INSIGHT

Openness to critique not only improves performance—it builds a culture of continuous growth.

REFLECTION QUESTION

How can constructive feedback reshape my strategy today?

Day 172

I invest in my future
by continuously
learning and adapting.

INSIGHT

Growth never stops; each lesson deepens your capacity to lead and innovate.

REFLECTION QUESTION

What new learning can I integrate into my approach today?

Day 173

I reflect honestly on my progress and my missteps.

INSIGHT

Every experience, whether triumphant or challenging, is a tool for refining my leadership and understanding who I am.

REFLECTION QUESTION

What lesson have I learned from a recent misstep?

Day 174

I value the insights gained by embracing my strengths and weaknesses.

INSIGHT

Recognizing my imperfections fosters resilience and clears the way for genuine self-improvement.

REFLECTION QUESTION

How can embracing my limitations open up opportunities for growth?

Day 175

I balance honest self-assessment with gentle self-compassion.

INSIGHT

Caring for myself as I learn helps maintain momentum without succumbing to harsh criticism.

REFLECTION QUESTION

How can I support myself when I fall short of my expectations?

Part 5

Focusing on What Matters

"Making decisions from a centered place."

Day 176

I schedule my calendar to reflect my leadership priorities.

INSIGHT

What gets scheduled gets done. Structure your time to reflect what you truly value.

REFLECTION QUESTION

Where am I spending time that doesn't align with my priorities?

Day 177

I protect time for what matters most.

INSIGHT

Distraction is the enemy of intention. If you don't guard your focus, someone else will fill it. Prioritizing isn't about doing more—it's about doing what counts.

REFLECTION QUESTION

Is my calendar aligned with my values and goals?

Day 178

I focus on impact, not attention.

INSIGHT

Leadership isn't about visibility, it's about results. Recognition fades, but impact lasts. Keep your energy aligned with purpose, not applause.

REFLECTION QUESTION

Am I prioritizing visibility or value in my leadership approach?

Day 179

I take small,
purposeful steps to
realign my vision.

INSIGHT

Leadership isn't only about bold moves. Tiny choices, daily discipline, and quiet consistency carry the vision forward—often more powerfully than declarations.

REFLECTION QUESTION

What small act today supports the future I'm building?

Day 180

I center purpose in
every decision.

INSIGHT

Busy days can cloud your mission. When you reconnect to the "why" behind your choices, you move from reaction to alignment.

REFLECTION QUESTION

What purpose is guiding my work today?

Day 181

I provide clear direction to build my team's confidence.

INSIGHT

People don't need perfection—they need clarity. Vision paired with direction creates a sense of safety, motivation, and progress.

REFLECTION QUESTION

What next step needs to be clarified for the team?

Day 182

*I focus my energy on
what truly matters.*

INSIGHT

In a world full of distractions, discerning what
truly matters allows me to focus my energy
where it counts. That focus is a choice, one
that requires boundaries, clarity, and courage.
When I align my actions with my core values, I
lead with intention instead of obligation.

REFLECTION QUESTION

What commitment today best reflects my core
purpose, and what might I need to release to
honor it?

Day 183

I create clarity,

starting with myself.

INSIGHT

If my team is confused, I start by examining how I communicate. Clarity isn't about intelligence—it's a reflection of leadership. When I speak with intention and make the vision visible, I help others move with confidence, not guesswork.

REFLECTION QUESTION

What message or goal needs clearer direction from me today?

Day 184

I plant seeds where

growth matters most.

INSIGHT

Not every task needs your full attention. Effective leaders prioritize by investing in the people, projects, and practices that align with their values. Choosing where to plant your energy is how you lead with focus—not control.

REFLECTION QUESTION

Where am I choosing to invest my energy for meaningful growth today?

Day 185

I choose what matters, even when it's not urgent.

INSIGHT

Not everything loud is important. Discernment means focusing on what will make a difference beyond today's noise. When I prioritize what truly matters, I lead with clarity, not reactivity.

REFLECTION QUESTION

What meaningful priority am I choosing to protect today?

Day 186

I turn vision into progress through clear goal.

INSIGHT

Big dreams fade without small steps. When I set clear goals, I give my vision structure, direction, and momentum. Goals aren't about pressure, they're how I move purposefully toward what matters..

REFLECTION QUESTION

What goal needs to be redefined, or recommitted to, this week

Day 187

I rally focus by naming the goal that matters most.

INSIGHT

When direction is unclear, momentum fades. By identifying and articulating the right goal, I help my team realign, refocus, and move with shared purpose..

REFLECTION QUESTION

What goal do we need to re-center around this month?

Day 188

I lead with clarity—
especially when things
get murky.

INSIGHT

Clarity isn't a bonus—it's a basic need. When I make direction and expectations clear, I reduce confusion and build trust. It starts with what I choose to say and how I say it.

REFLECTION QUESTION

Where has clarity slipped, and what can I do about it?

Day 189

I ground my day in
one clear goal.

INSIGHT

When life feels chaotic, clarity creates calm. Even one focused goal can anchor my energy and help me move forward with purpose, not overwhelm.

REFLECTION QUESTION

What small, clear goal can anchor me today?

Day 190

I return to clear goals when the work feels messy.

INSIGHT

When things feel uncertain or chaotic, a well-defined goal can ground your actions and renew your focus. Re-centering brings direction back into reach. Revisit them. Refocus. Then act.

REFLECTION QUESTION

What goal needs to be re-centered right now?

Day 191

I share clear goals to
inspire possibility.

INSIGHT

When I make goals visible, I help others see
what's possible—not just for me, but for us.
Clarity creates momentum. It turns vision into
something others can believe in and contribute
to.

REFLECTION QUESTION

Who might find new energy or direction if I
made the goal clearer today?

Day 192

I lead with clarity so others can lead with confidence.

INSIGHT

Vague goals and shifting expectations create anxiety. Clarity gives your team freedom—not restriction. It sets the direction, then lets people move.

REFLECTION QUESTION

What's one decision or direction I need to clarify for others?

Day 193

*I set clear expectations
to support those I lead.*

INSIGHT

Clarity is an act of care. When people know
what success looks like, they feel safer, more
confident, and more empowered. Ambiguity
creates stress—clear expectations create
trust.

REFLECTION QUESTION

Where can I offer more clarity to ease pressure
or uncertainty?

Day 194

I mentor to multiply impact.

INSIGHT

When I invest in others, I extend the reach of my leadership. Mentoring isn't about having all the answers—it's about creating space for growth, confidence, and shared purpose to take root and thrive..

REFLECTION QUESTION

Who could benefit from a conversation about their potential?

Day 195

I pay attention to patterns that reveal what I truly value.

INSIGHT

What I repeat, intentionally or not, shapes how others experience my leadership. Patterns in how I lead, decide, and respond speak louder than intentions. If something feels off, I start by noticing what I've been reinforcing..

REFLECTION QUESTION

What recent pattern might be reflecting a value I need to realign?

Day 196

I honor the quiet work that keeps things strong.

INSIGHT

Not every contribution gets attention, but that doesn't mean it lacks impact. When I stay steady, hold space, or offer quiet care, I'm reinforcing what makes lasting leadership possible.

REFLECTION QUESTION

What work have I done lately that mattered, even if no one noticed?

Day 197

I make small, steady changes that build real momentum.

INSIGHT

Sustainable change doesn't always come from bold moves. Often, it's the small, consistent adjustments that shift culture, improve systems, and build trust over time.

REFLECTION QUESTION

What small change can I make today to move us in the right direction?

Day 198

I inspire by staying connected to what matters.

INSIGHT

Inspiration isn't performance, it's alignment. When you live your values, others feel invited to do the same.

REFLECTION QUESTION

What part of my life or work could reignite my own inspiration?

Day 199

I communicate with clarity so others can move forward.

INSIGHT

People don't need perfection from me—they need direction. When I speak with clarity and honesty, I make progress possible. Assuming understanding creates confusion. Confirming it creates momentum.

REFLECTION QUESTION

Where do I need to clarify the message before expecting movement?

Day 200

I lead from within,
guided by purpose
over pressure.

INSIGHT

In a world full of noise, clarity begins with reconnecting to your core. When you lead from your values, decisions become clearer, and distractions lose their power.

REFLECTION QUESTION

What value will I return to today to guide my next decision?

Day 201

I challenge outdated systems to create lasting impact.

INSIGHT

When you see inefficiencies, your willingness to address them can spark long-term change. True leadership questions the status quo to build better structures.

REFLECTION QUESTION

Which process or system in my work needs rethinking, and why?

I set a clear internal foundation from which all action flows.

INSIGHT

When your inner purpose is defined, every decision takes on new clarity and direction.

REFLECTION QUESTION

Which of my core values guides my actions most consistently?

Day 203

I observe the systems
that shape my world
and use them as tools
for improvement.

INSIGHT

A reflective eye on systems reveals opportunities for lasting change.

REFLECTION QUESTION

What process in my life could benefit from a fresh perspective?

Day 204

I lead with clarity and conviction, setting a steady course for the future.

INSIGHT

When you communicate clear, value-driven direction, others follow not out of obligation but out of shared vision.

REFLECTION QUESTION

What clear message can I deliver today that aligns with my long-term vision?

Day 205

I challenge old habits

to uncover new

opportunities.

INSIGHT

By questioning the status quo in my daily practices, I open doors to innovative improvements in my leadership.

REFLECTION QUESTION

What habit or routine could I rethink to foster positive change?

Day 206

I refine my processes to better serve my long-term aspirations.

INSIGHT

Continuous improvement in how I operate today sets the stage for tomorrow's achievements.

REFLECTION QUESTION

What is one refinement I can make to my daily process for long-term benefit?

Day 207

I challenge outdated habits to create space for innovation.

INSIGHT

Reexamining and refining your processes can reveal new opportunities for growth and efficiency.

REFLECTION QUESTION

What habitual practice needs a fresh perspective to better support my vision?

Day 208

I step forward with clear intent, knowing the future is built one decision at a time.

INSIGHT

Each choice I make shapes the direction I'm leading—not just for today, but for what comes next. Intentional decisions create alignment, momentum, and trust over time.

REFLECTION QUESTION

What one decision today will shape the path for my future leadership?

Day 209

I align my daily actions with a clear, evolving vision.

INSIGHT

Every choice contributes to a larger narrative of who I am and where I'm heading; clarity in my actions molds my future.

REFLECTION QUESTION

How does my routine reflect the bigger picture I aim to create?

Day 210

I release what no longer serves the mission.

INSIGHT

Sustainability means letting go as much as pressing forward. If a process, belief, or habit no longer fits, it's time to make space.

REFLECTION QUESTION

What do I need to release to move forward well?

Day 211

I measure progress by meaning, not just metrics.

INSIGHT

The most important shifts aren't always quantifiable. Trust, care, and culture grow quietly—yet they sustain everything else.

REFLECTION QUESTION

What meaningful progress am I overlooking?

Day 212

I stay rooted when things get noisy.

INSIGHT

Distractions are constant. Stay grounded in what matters most. Your presence cuts through the noise.

REFLECTION QUESTION

What helps me stay rooted amid distractions?

Day 213

I return to the purpose,
not the pressure.

INSIGHT

It's easy to get caught in urgency. Returning to your "why" keeps your work meaningful, grounded, and clear.

REFLECTION QUESTION

What purpose do I want to return to today?

Day 214

I value steady over

shiny.

INSIGHT

New isn't always better. Often, it's the steady effort and quiet consistency that builds what lasts.

REFLECTION QUESTION

Where have I undervalued the steady work?

Day 215

I lead from within—
every day, every
decision.

INSIGHT

Leadership isn't a title or a task list. It's how you carry your values through the decisions, conversations, and quiet moments of each day.

REFLECTION QUESTION

How will I live my leadership today, even in the ordinary?

Part 6

Aligning Systems with Purpose

"Aligning your environment with your values."

Day 216

I see systems, not just symptoms.

INSIGHT

Chronic problems often come from structural roots. Great leaders look beyond the immediate issue to examine the patterns, processes, and blind spots that created it.

REFLECTION QUESTION

What larger pattern might be underneath this recurring issue?

Day 217

I create structures that support, not control.

INSIGHT

Empowering systems don't over-direct; they create space for initiative and clarity. Good structures act like scaffolding: strong, flexible, and built to come down.

REFLECTION QUESTION

What structure is helping—or hindering—my team's growth?

Day 218

I make space for tension without rushing resolution.

INSIGHT

Quick fixes often mask deeper misalignments. Holding space for honest discomfort can lead to wiser, longer-lasting change.

REFLECTION QUESTION

What tension deserves more listening and less fixing?

Day 219

I design systems
knowing every process
reshapes culture.

INSIGHT

Culture isn't what's written, it's what's repeated. Change the habits, rhythms, and processes. The culture will follow, whether you mean to or not.

REFLECTION QUESTION

What system do I influence, and what could a healthier version look like?

Day 220

I shape systems that

will shape the future.

INSIGHT

Even quiet policies carry forward your values. When you lead with integrity, your systems echo it for years to come.

REFLECTION QUESTION

What future am I designing through today's structures?

Day 221

My leadership includes the systems I build and protect.

INSIGHT

Build structures that support the culture you want. It's not just what you do—it's what you defend. Systems that reflect justice and clarity need active protection from drift, decay, or distortion.

REFLECTION QUESTION

What system needs to shift to align with what I believe?

Day 222

I foster an environment of collaborative innovation.

INSIGHT

Innovation thrives when ideas are shared freely within clear frameworks, where roles shift, and creativity is supported, not scattered.

REFLECTION QUESTION

What kind of system would make creativity and collaboration the default?

Day 223

*I view my daily
routines as building
blocks of culture.*

INSIGHT

Culture doesn't start with vision statements; it starts with how we begin meetings, handle mistakes, and make room for rest. Daily structure becomes moral architecture.

REFLECTION QUESTION

What daily rhythm reinforces what I truly value?

Day 224

I design my daily routines to support my long-term vision.

INSIGHT

Intentional systems ensure that your everyday actions contribute toward a meaningful future.

REFLECTION QUESTION

Which daily routine aligns most with my future goals, and how can I strengthen it?

Day 225

I design my routines to reflect my values.

INSIGHT

What I repeat becomes what I believe. My daily habits speak louder than any statement of values. When I shape my routines with intention, I lead from alignment, not autopilot.

REFLECTION QUESTION

Which routine am I redesigning to better reflect what matters most?

Day 226

I act with awareness of how each choice shapes the future we share.

INSIGHT

Every decision—no matter how small—carries weight beyond the moment. When you lead with intention, you help shape a future that reflects your values, not just your goals. Leadership is about understanding your influence and using it with care.

REFLECTION QUESTION

How does my action today integrate into my overall vision for tomorrow?

Day 227

I build what others can build on.

INSIGHT

Lasting leadership creates a foundation, not a monument. Make it easier for others to go farther because of the way you lead now.

REFLECTION QUESTION

What am I leaving behind that makes the work better for others?

Day 228

I build with clarity and care, knowing what I create will carry forward.

INSIGHT

My values live in what I design, not just in what I say. When I create structures or habits with clarity and fairness, I shape an environment that can thrive even when I step away.

REFLECTION QUESTION

What habit or structure am I shaping today, and what does it reflect about my values?

Day 229

I design systems that reflect my values.

INSIGHT

Every structure you create—from meetings to workflows—teaches people what matters. Build with intention.

REFLECTION QUESTION

What current system could better reflect our core values?

I build thoughtful systems that make great work possible.

INSIGHT

When structure is clear and intentional, it frees up energy for creativity, focus, and momentum. I reduce friction by designing systems that support, not distract from, the work that matters.

REFLECTION QUESTION

What friction point could I address with a more effective process or structure?

Day 231

I use structure to support, not to control.

INSIGHT

Systems that lift people are better than systems that limit them. Build with flexibility, not rigidity.

REFLECTION QUESTION

What process might benefit from more trust and less oversight?

Day 232

I bring clarity to the process so others can lead with confidence.

INSIGHT

For many, understanding the "how" unlocks their courage to engage with the "why." Process clarity isn't about control—it's about empowerment. When I make the path clear, I help others step into leadership.

REFLECTION QUESTION

Where could a clearer process empower others to lead?

Day 233

I don't just fix problems I build better systems.

INSIGHT

Solving symptoms is short-term. Real leadership identifies the root and re-engineers the process so the problem doesn't come back.

REFLECTION QUESTION

What issue might be a sign of a broken system?

Day 234

I ask what the system is rewarding.

INSIGHT

Every system reinforces something—urgency, silence, independence, collaboration. Make sure it's what you intend.

REFLECTION QUESTION

What outcome is my current system encouraging—and is it the right one?

Day 235

I build rhythms that renew and restore.

INSIGHT

Healthy systems include space for rest, not just output. Leadership is sustainable when recovery is part of the plan.

REFLECTION QUESTION

What rhythm do I need to reset to avoid burnout?

Day 236

I lead through design,

not just direction.

INSIGHT

Leadership isn't just about vision; it's about structure. Thoughtful design reinforces clarity more powerfully than any speech.

REFLECTION QUESTION

What structure might say more than my words?

Day 237

I create structures that adapt, not just sustain.

INSIGHT

Great systems aren't frozen; they flex. Resilient design includes room for learning, evolving, and rebalancing.

REFLECTION QUESTION

Where could adaptability strengthen our current process?

Day 238

I lead with consistency to build trust that lasts.

INSIGHT

Trust grows from predictable processes. When people can rely on how things work, they free up energy for creativity, not second-guessing. My consistency sets the tone for confidence and clarity.

REFLECTION QUESTION

What part of our structure builds or breaks trust?

Day 239

I align structure with strategy.

INSIGHT

Vision without infrastructure is just a dream. When structure and strategy reinforce each other, momentum becomes sustainable.

REFLECTION QUESTION

Does our structure support our strategy, or get in the way?

Day 240

I review what I've built
so it can keep
improving.

INSIGHT

Systems aren't "set and forget." Regular reflection helps you spot where even good structures have stopped serving their purpose and when it's time to evolve.

REFLECTION QUESTION

What system is overdue for a thoughtful review?

Day 241

I make time to strengthen the foundation.

INSIGHT

Urgency hides weakness. When you slow down to reinforce the basics—communication, clarity, and equity—your system becomes more resilient to crises.

REFLECTION QUESTION

What foundational system deserves more attention right now?

Day 242

I shape systems that

serve people.

INSIGHT

Structure exists to support people, not the other way around. Human-centered design fosters a sense of belonging and trust.

REFLECTION QUESTION

Who benefits from this system—and who might it leave behind?

Day 243

I design systems that accurately reflect the message I intend to send.

INSIGHT

How we structure time, decisions, and access tells people what we value. Make sure it speaks clearly.

REFLECTION QUESTION

What message is my structure sending, whether I intended it or not?

Day 244

I make systems more humane by making them more honest.

INSIGHT

Transparency builds trust. Even the best-designed system fails if it reveals less than it conceals.

REFLECTION QUESTION

Where could greater transparency improve the system's effectiveness?

*My systems reflect
how I lead when I'm
not in the room.*

INSIGHT

The true test of leadership isn't presence, it's process. What you've built will either empower or confuse.

REFLECTION QUESTION

What does this system allow others to do—or prevent them from doing—when I'm not there?

Day 246

I simplify with purpose
so others can move
with confidence.

INSIGHT

Complexity creates friction. When my systems are simple, clear, and purposeful, they make action easier, not harder. Simplicity isn't a shortcut; it's a strategy for clarity and momentum.

REFLECTION QUESTION

What process could be simplified to create more clarity and momentum?

Day 247

I build systems that make good decisions easier.

INSIGHT

Don't leave critical values up to chance. Build a structure that reinforces what matters most, especially under pressure.

REFLECTION QUESTION

What values should our system make easier to live out?

Day 248

I reflect to redesign.

INSIGHT

When something feels off, don't just push harder. Step back, assess the structure, and refine what's underneath.

REFLECTION QUESTION

What system might be causing the friction I'm feeling?

Day 249

I adapt systems to meet the needs of those we serve.

INSIGHT

Growth means outgrowing old structures. When a system no longer fits the people it's meant to support, it's time to redesign, not just retrain. Outdated systems lead to disengagement.

REFLECTION QUESTION

What shift in our people needs a shift in our systems?

Day 250

I track progress to support growth, not to control it.

INSIGHT

Metrics should guide, not punish. When data is used for curiosity and improvement, it becomes a tool for care, not control.

REFLECTION QUESTION

Are we using data to empower—or to micromanage?

Day 251

I build in time for maintenance not just momentum.

INSIGHT

Even high-functioning systems need tending. Without care, great structures wear down or break.

REFLECTION QUESTION

What regular check-in would help our systems stay strong?

Day 252

I use structure to

create freedom.

INSIGHT

The right guardrails don't restrict; they unlock. Clear boundaries and rhythms reduce decision fatigue, freeing people to lead boldly.

REFLECTION QUESTION

What boundary or system could free up energy for creativity or care?

Day 253

I treat every change I make to systems as a leadership decision.

INSIGHT

Small edits to a process ripple outward. Changing a template, meeting structure, or norm is a message. Make it intentional. Every tweak tells a story.

REFLECTION QUESTION

What story does this change tell about who we are becoming?

Day 254

I shape culture

through process.

INSIGHT

Culture isn't built in slogans, it's built in what we repeat without thinking. Leaders don't just set culture with words. They shape it every day through the processes they reinforce and the behaviors they model.

REFLECTION QUESTION

What part of our culture is being quietly shaped by systems I've never questioned?

My systems are quiet teachers of what I believe.

INSIGHT

People learn from how your calendar works, how decisions are made, and how conflict is handled. Systems teach, so teach well.

REFLECTION QUESTION

What is one system I lead that could model more justice, clarity, or trust?

Part 7

Building Others Up

"Growing people, not just outcomes."

Day 256

I create space for others to lead.

INSIGHT

Leadership isn't control; it's cultivation. Step back, and you'll often see someone else step forward.

REFLECTION QUESTION

Where can I step aside to let someone else step forward?

Day 257

I prepare the way,
even if I don't walk it.

INSIGHT

Legacy isn't just about what you build. It's also about how you prepare others to build after you. When you lead with humility, you create a foundation others can stand on.

REFLECTION QUESTION

What am I doing now that could make the way easier for someone else?

Day 258

*I lead with the next
leader in mind.*

INSIGHT

Good leaders shine. Great ones prepare others
to do the same. Your job isn't to be
irreplaceable, it's to make others ready.

REFLECTION QUESTION

Who will benefit from the groundwork I lay
today?

Day 259

I guide others to lead beyond me.

INSIGHT

Leadership isn't about keeping others dependent, it's about building capacity that lasts.

REFLECTION QUESTION

Who am I preparing to lead without me?

Day 260

I help others find their voice.

INSIGHT

The best legacy isn't your echo—it's the chorus of leaders you've helped rise. Make space for voices that haven't been heard yet.

REFLECTION QUESTION

Who needs encouragement to lead in their own way?

Day 261

I create safe space for others to grow with confidence.

INSIGHT

People grow best in environments of trust and autonomy. Letting go of control isn't withdrawal, it's an invitation. When growth is supported, not rushed or judged, people rise on their own terms.

REFLECTION QUESTION

How can I offer more trust or safety so someone else can grow more freely?

Day 261

I lead with presence,

not pressure.

INSIGHT

You don't need to be forceful to be effective. Calm, grounded presence creates trust and space for others to grow.

REFLECTION QUESTION

How can I bring steadiness instead of urgency?

Day 262

I name what's working.

INSIGHT

Recognition fuels resilience. Take time to name the small wins; they remind your team and yourself, that progress is real.

REFLECTION QUESTION

What's one thing that's going well right now?

Day 263

I don't lead alone.

INSIGHT

The myth of the solo leader wears people down. Sustainable leadership is relational, it's built in partnership, support, and shared capacity.

REFLECTION QUESTION

Who can I lean on this week, and how can I support them, too?

Day 264

I create a safe space
for others to grow with
confidence.

INSIGHT

People grow best in environments of trust and autonomy. Letting go of control isn't withdrawal, it's an invitation. When growth is supported, not rushed or judged, people rise on their own terms.

REFLECTION QUESTION

How can I offer more trust or safety so someone else can grow more freely?

Day 265

I leave space for others to grow even as I continue my own evolution.

INSIGHT

Leadership flourishes when I empower others to rise alongside me, fostering an environment of mutual growth and development.

REFLECTION QUESTION

How can I create more opportunities for others to step into leadership roles today?

Day 266

I empower others through my quiet strength.

INSIGHT

Strength doesn't always shout. The steady presence of someone who believes in you can change your story.

REFLECTION QUESTION

What small act of empowerment can I offer someone today?

Day 267

I empower others by investing in their development.

INSIGHT

True leadership is measured by the strength and growth of those you uplift. Your mentorship plants seeds for a brighter future.

REFLECTION QUESTION

Who can I support today to help cultivate their leadership potential?

Day 268

I build bridges through every conversation I engage in.

INSIGHT

Trust is built in dialogue. A single conversation, approached with care, can change how people feel about themselves—and you.

REFLECTION QUESTION

Which conversation today can be an opportunity to build a stronger connection?

Day 269

I welcome vulnerability as an invitation to learn.

INSIGHT

When you can admit you don't have all the answers, you build trust. Real strength comes from honesty, not pretending to have it all figured out.

REFLECTION QUESTION

What recent moment of vulnerability has taught me something about connection?

Day 270

I lead with humility, owning both my strengths and limits.

INSIGHT

You don't need all the answers. Humble leadership invites trust, learning, and authentic connection.

REFLECTION QUESTION

How can I show humility in my decisions and interactions today?

Day 271

I empower others by inviting them to share my load.

INSIGHT

Shared responsibility builds trust and resilience. Delegation isn't about giving tasks, it's about giving trust.

REFLECTION QUESTION

Where might I delegate or share responsibility to build strength in others?

Day 272

I mentor by showing up, not just speaking up.

INSIGHT

People don't always need direction. Sometimes they need to know they're not alone. Mentorship is often more about walking beside than pointing ahead.

REFLECTION QUESTION

How can I show up today as a mentor through presence, not just instruction?

Day 273

I lead with humility,

not as weakness, but

as strength.

INSIGHT

Humility is knowing your influence without needing to prove it. It allows you to listen, grow, and earn trust. People follow leaders who serve, not boast.

REFLECTION QUESTION

What might humility teach me in this moment?

Day 274

I mentor others with what I've learned.

INSIGHT

Your wisdom is a gift meant to be passed on. When you share lessons, you shorten the learning curve for others.

REFLECTION QUESTION

Who might benefit from a story I haven't shared yet?

Day 275

I trust others to rise

when given the chance.

INSIGHT

Empowerment means letting go of control. When you trust people with real responsibility, they grow, and so does your capacity as a leader.

REFLECTION QUESTION

Who needs more trust and autonomy from me?

Day 276

I lead in ways that help others see their own potential.

INSIGHT

Great leadership isn't about being the center of attention. It's about creating conditions where others feel confident, capable, and ready to contribute. Empowerment happens when people feel seen and believed in.

REFLECTION QUESTION

Who might see more in themselves if I led with encouragement and belief?

Day 277

I know when to lead
and when to listen.

INSIGHT

Wisdom isn't loud. Knowing when to step back is just as powerful as knowing when to speak up.

REFLECTION QUESTION

What's one moment I can lead by stepping back this week?

Day 278

Even small encouragement can change a day.

INSIGHT

Kindness costs little but builds much. A word of support, recognition, or belief can change someone's mindset and their performance.

REFLECTION QUESTION

Who might need encouragement I haven't given yet?

Day 279

I give others the credit they've earned.

INSIGHT

People grow in the light of recognition. When you share the spotlight, you build trust and elevate those around you.

REFLECTION QUESTION

Who deserves more recognition than I've given?

Day 280

*I lead today so others
can lead tomorrow.*

INSIGHT

Lasting leadership isn't about holding power—
it's about growing it in others. The leaders you
raise today will carry your values forward
tomorrow.

REFLECTION QUESTION

How am I preparing others to lead beyond me?

Day 281

I create space for ideas that aren't mine.

INSIGHT

Innovation grows when many voices contribute. Good leaders invite brilliance, not just deliver it. Letting others lead the thinking fosters innovation and ownership.

REFLECTION QUESTION

How am I creating room for other voices to lead?

I lead with humility so others can rise.

INSIGHT

Humility in power means prioritizing the collective, not the spotlight. Your restraint can amplify someone else's growth.

REFLECTION QUESTION

Where can I hold back so someone else can step forward?

Day 283

I let people grow in their own time, not mine.

INSIGHT

Growth isn't always on your timeline. True support allows others to unfold at the pace that's right for them.

REFLECTION QUESTION

Where am I confusing support with pressure?

Day 284

I don't lead to fix, I lead to support growth.

INSIGHT

Your role isn't to rescue, it's to resource. When you build capacity instead of control, you create leaders instead of followers.

REFLECTION QUESTION

Where can I step back to let growth happen?

Day 285

I amplify others so their strengths are seen and valued.

INSIGHT

Leadership isn't diminished by visibility—it's expanded by generosity. When you lift others up, you create a culture where success is shared, and confidence takes root.

REFLECTION QUESTION

How can I help someone else feel seen and celebrated today?

Day 286

I build leaders, not followers.

INSIGHT

Leadership isn't about gathering followers, it's about building others' confidence and capacity. When people are trusted, guided, and empowered, leadership multiplies.

REFLECTION QUESTION

Whose leadership have I helped develop this month, and how might I support their next step?

Day 287

I lead so others can lead.

INSIGHT

Leadership isn't about being the center, it's about creating capacity. Your strength is in what you empower others to do, not just what you accomplish.

REFLECTION QUESTION

What opportunity can I give to someone else today?

Day 288

My voice is one of many, and that's strength.

INSIGHT

Leadership that centers community invites shared wisdom. When decisions are shaped by many, outcomes are more sustainable—and more just.

REFLECTION QUESTION

Where can I make space for more voices in the outcome?

Day 289

*I invest in people, not
just performance.*

INSIGHT

Projects finish. People grow. True leadership
shapes people who will go on to shape others.

REFLECTION QUESTION

Whose growth am I nurturing intentionally?

Day 290

I lift others now so they can rise long after I'm gone.

INSIGHT

Empowerment isn't about recognition—it's about continuity. When you nurture others with care and intention, your influence becomes a foundation they can build on.

REFLECTION QUESTION

Who am I empowering today in ways that may only be fully seen tomorrow?

Part 8

Leading with Endurance and Balance

"Endurance with integrity."

Day 291

I recharge to remain reliable.

INSIGHT

Sustainability in leadership requires rest. You can't be steady for others if you don't restore yourself.

REFLECTION QUESTION

What small habit can I adopt to restore my energy and focus this week?

Day 292

I honor the seasons of

my leadership.

INSIGHT

Leadership isn't a linear ascent. Some seasons are for growth, others for rest, recalibration, or healing. Name the season, and lead accordingly.

REFLECTION QUESTION

What season am I in, and how can I honor it rather than resist it?

Day 293

I check in with myself before I check off the list.

INSIGHT

Productivity without awareness quickly gives way to burnout. When you pause to notice how you feel, before the doing begins, you lead from a grounded, present place that honors both task and self.

REFLECTION QUESTION

How am I really doing right now?

Day 294

I rest with intention,

not guilt.

INSIGHT

Rest isn't a break from responsibility—it's how you remain responsible. It's not selfish to recharge. It's necessary. Guilt has no place in the healing process.

REFLECTION QUESTION

What kind of rest do I actually need right now?

Day 295

I don't have to be at my best to still be a good leader.

INSIGHT

Leadership isn't a performance, it's a presence. Some days will be harder than others. Show up with honesty, even if you're not at 100%. Grace for yourself is part of the grace you offer others

REFLECTION QUESTION

How can I show up today with what I have, not what I wish I had?

Day 296

I strengthen my inner reserves to lead with resilience.

INSIGHT

The strength to endure doesn't come from willpower alone; it comes from within. Practices like reflection, rest, and spiritual grounding replenish the well of leadership.

REFLECTION QUESTION

How can I further strengthen my internal resolve in the face of today's challenges?

Day 297

My presence can reduce anxiety, even when I don't have answers.

INSIGHT

People don't always need solutions. They need steadiness. When you stay grounded, others feel safe enough to think clearly.

REFLECTION QUESTION

How can I bring calm into a space that feels tense?

Day 298

I offer clarity in chaos.

INSIGHT

When everything feels uncertain, your clarity becomes a gift. Clear communication calms both your nervous system and that of others. It's not perfection that people need, but grounded direction.

REFLECTION QUESTION

What's one thing I can clarify today?

Day 299

I lead with clarity that liberates, not controls.

INSIGHT

Clear communication lightens the load for everyone. When you define direction and expectations well, you reduce confusion, prevent over-functioning, and protect your own energy. Clarity becomes a boundary that sustains both you and your team.

REFLECTION QUESTION

What expectations or goals could I restate more clearly to empower others?

Day 300

I set the tone through the presence I choose to bring.

INSIGHT

You don't need to speak to influence a room. The energy you bring—calm, tense, grounded, distracted—sets the rhythm for others.

REFLECTION QUESTION

What energy am I carrying into the spaces I lead?

Day 301

I resolve conflict

without erasing

complexity.

INSIGHT

Not all conflicts have a clean solution. Wise leadership means holding space for discomfort, staying present through tension, and honoring the humanity in everyone, even when resolution is slow.

REFLECTION QUESTION

What complex tension am I willing to hold with compassion today?

Day 302

I allow myself to be human.

INSIGHT

Leadership doesn't require you to be invincible. You're allowed to rest, reflect, make mistakes, and keep moving forward.

REFLECTION QUESTION

Where do I need to offer myself more compassion today?

Day 303

When I slow down, I lead better.

INSIGHT

Stillness is a strength. Space lets you see patterns. Don't confuse motion with momentum.

REFLECTION QUESTION

Where can I slow the pace to lead with more depth?

Day 304

I rest before I burn out.

INSIGHT

You don't prove your value by draining yourself. When you rest early and regularly, you model a leadership rooted in wisdom, not martyrdom. Renewal is part of responsibility.

REFLECTION QUESTION

Am I leading the way I'd want my team to live?

Day 305

I use clarity to create courage.

INSIGHT

When direction is clear, fear begins to fade. People feel braver when they know what's expected, where they're going, and that they're not alone. Clarity is a kindness that strengthens others.

REFLECTION QUESTION

How can I make the next step clearer for someone else?

Day 306

I honor the rhythm of growth—steady, slow, and real.

INSIGHT

Leadership isn't a sprint. It unfolds over time, shaped by intention and consistency. When you stop measuring success by speed and start measuring by depth, you create space for meaningful, sustainable progress.

REFLECTION QUESTION

Where might a slower, steadier pace support deeper growth?

Day 307

I lead better when I'm rested.

INSIGHT

You can't pour from an empty cup. Leadership without rest becomes reactive and narrow. Rest protects your clarity and your compassion.

REFLECTION QUESTION

Where can I build recovery into my routine this week?

Day 308

I use obstacles as opportunities to build resilience.

INSIGHT

Challenges don't just test you—they shape you. When you meet difficulty with purpose and reflection, you grow stronger in ways that sustain you and support those you lead who depend on your steadiness.

REFLECTION QUESTION

What strength am I gaining through this challenge?

Day 309

My presence invites stability.

INSIGHT

Leadership is as much about how you carry yourself as what you say. In times of instability, people seek something solid. When you lead with presence, others begin to steady themselves as well.

REFLECTION QUESTION

How can I offer stability through my presence today?

Day 310

I stay steady, even
when things get loud.

INSIGHT

Not all leadership is visible. Sometimes, it's your steadiness, your breath, and your presence that anchor a room. You don't have to shout to be a leader.

REFLECTION QUESTION

Where can I hold space instead of filling it?

Day 311

I return to my values
when the path gets
unclear.

INSIGHT

In moments of uncertainty, values serve as your compass. You don't need to have every answer, but when you lead from your principles, your next step becomes clearer.

REFLECTION QUESTION

What value do I need to come back to today?

Day 312

Calm is a gift I can offer any room.

INSIGHT

You don't always need the answers to bring value. Sometimes, just being grounded and present helps others breathe more deeply and think more clearly.

REFLECTION QUESTION

Where could my calm shift the tone of a conversation or space?

Day 313

I lead through the storm, not just the calm.

INSIGHT

Leadership isn't proven when everything's going right. It's revealed when things fall apart. Your steadiness during challenging moments helps others hold their own.

REFLECTION QUESTION

What does calm leadership look like for me in times of stress?

Day 314

I rest without guilt.

INSIGHT

Rest is not a detour from meaningful work—it is a form of devotion to it. By allowing yourself to rest, you affirm your dignity, nourish your resilience, and model a sustainable path for others to follow.

REFLECTION QUESTION

How can I rest this week in a way that strengthens my leadership?

Day 315

I slow down so I can lead with clarity.

INSIGHT

In a world that praises speed, slowing down is a radical act. It allows you to notice what others miss, to respond instead of react, and to lead with the grounded wisdom that only stillness can offer.

REFLECTION QUESTION

What could slowing down help me see more clearly?

Day 316

I lead with presence,
even when I say
nothing.

INSIGHT

Your body language, attention, and tone say as much as your words. Leadership is as much felt as heard. Even silence can build—or break—trust.

REFLECTION QUESTION

What is my presence communicating today?

I hold the weight of leadership without letting it crush me.

INSIGHT

The pressure is real. But perspective, boundaries, and support are what keep it from becoming unbearable. You don't have to carry everything alone.

REFLECTION QUESTION

What am I holding right now—and what do I need to let go of?

Day 318

I release urgency so I can lead with clarity.

INSIGHT

Urgency pulls us out of wisdom and into reactivity. When you slow down and breathe, you create the space to discern rather than react, and that space becomes a source of wise, grounded leadership.

REFLECTION QUESTION

Where is urgency pushing me, and what might clarity choose instead?

Day 319

Even in stillness, I

lead.

INSIGHT

Leadership doesn't always look like motion. Pausing to reflect, listen, or breathe often has more impact than reacting.

REFLECTION QUESTION

What moment today deserves my pause?

Day 320

I make time to refill what's been poured out.

INSIGHT

You give so much to others—strategy, care, direction. Refilling is not selfish. Make space to receive, too. What fills you fuels you.

REFLECTION QUESTION

What do I need more of to stay grounded and generous?

Day 321

I lead with a calm and balanced heart, grounded in my truth.

INSIGHT

When inner calm prevails, my actions are both deliberate and compassionate, reflecting the leader I aspire to be.

REFLECTION QUESTION

How can I nurture my inner balance to influence my decisions today?

Day 322

I protect my energy to lead with purpose, not depletion.

INSIGHT

Energy and attention aren't infinite. When you lead without replenishing, clarity and compassion fade. Protecting your energy isn't selfish. It sustains your ability to serve with purpose and presence.

REFLECTION QUESTION

What boundary or rhythm would help me lead with more intention and less depletion?

Day 323

I am more productive when I take time to rest.

INSIGHT

The work you do to sustain yourself is not separate from your leadership; it is the foundation of it. Rest allows you to recalibrate, restore your vision, and lead in ways that are whole, present, and wise.

REFLECTION QUESTION

What permission do I need to give myself around rest?

Day 324

I face conflict with
calm and clarity.

INSIGHT

Conflict is not the enemy of leadership. It's a
doorway to deeper truth. Meeting it with
presence and discernment allows you to
model courage and emotional wisdom in even
the most difficult conversations.

REFLECTION QUESTION

What conversation needs my calm attention
instead of my reaction?

Day 325

*I give myself
permission to pause.*

INSIGHT

Pausing isn't avoidance, it's awareness. It allows you to return to action with more clarity, steadiness, and integrity. A thoughtful pause can change the entire tone of your leadership.

REFLECTION QUESTION

Where could a pause help me lead more wisely?

Part 9

Leaving a Legacy

"Leading today with tomorrow in mind."

Day 326

I don't build a team for today; I build one for what comes next.

INSIGHT

Leadership is about what happens after you're gone. Invest in people not just for their current output, but for their potential to lead, grow, and guide others. That's how a legacy takes shape—in the people you've helped rise.

REFLECTION QUESTION

Whose leadership am I helping to grow right now?

Day 327

How I lead today

becomes someone

else's story tomorrow.

INSIGHT

The ripple effects of your leadership often reach farther than you'll ever see. Your steady presence today creates possibility for someone else.

REFLECTION QUESTION

What kind of leader will someone say I was, based on today?

Day 328

My legacy is built in moments of care.

INSIGHT

Ultimately, it's not about the metrics—it's about the people. Legacy lives in how you made others feel and what you helped them become.

REFLECTION QUESTION

Who might carry my leadership forward because I chose to care?

Day 329

I lead with the next generation in mind.

INSIGHT

Think beyond your timeline. Legacy means preparing the path, not just walking it.

REFLECTION QUESTION

How am I equipping others to lead beyond me?

Day 330

I lead by sharing my story, inviting others to learn and grow.

INSIGHT

Vulnerability in sharing personal experiences creates a bridge of understanding and fosters collective growth.

REFLECTION QUESTION

What part of my journey might inspire someone else if shared?

Day 331

*I leave a legacy
defined by thoughtful
actions, not fleeting
moments.*

INSIGHT

Legacy is built in the quiet details, in the follow-through, kindness, and presence. What you repeat matters more than what you declare.

REFLECTION QUESTION

What small act today will shape how I'm remembered tomorrow?

Day 332

I shape my legacy by practicing what I preach.

INSIGHT

Words matter—but behavior endures. When your values consistently show up in how you treat people, trust becomes your lasting legacy.

REFLECTION QUESTION

How are my actions today contributing to the legacy I wish to leave?

*I lead by inspiring
others to find their
own strength.*

INSIGHT

Leadership is not about making others follow—
it's about helping them rise. When you reflect
people's strength back to them, you leave
behind courage that lasts.

REFLECTION QUESTION

Who can I empower today to take a bold step
forward?

Day 334

I mentor not just with words, but through consistent action.

INSIGHT

Mentoring is shown in daily acts of care and competence. Your example plants the seeds for someone else's growth.

REFLECTION QUESTION

What recent action of mine has sparked growth in another?

Day 335

What I nurture in others becomes the living legacy of my leadership

INSIGHT

You may not be remembered by name, but your kindness, clarity, and presence live on in how others lead. Legacy isn't kept—it's carried forward.

REFLECTION QUESTION

Whose growth reflects the care I've given, even quietly?

Day 336

Legacy is the pattern of presence, repeated with care.

INSIGHT

Legacy isn't built in one defining act—it's formed in the small, consistent ways you show up over time. When your presence reflects your values again and again, it leaves a mark that outlasts you.

REFLECTION QUESTION

What repeated action today is shaping the memory of my leadership?

Day 337

I show up fully, even in small moments.

INSIGHT

Leadership is in the details: how you start meetings, how you respond to stress, how you hold silence. Every small act shapes trust.

REFLECTION QUESTION

What everyday moment could be a chance to lead well today?

Day 338

I lead through quiet consistency, not loud declarations.

INSIGHT

Legacy is built through daily steadiness. You don't need to announce your values, live them. The way you show up again and again speaks louder than any title or speech.

REFLECTION QUESTION

What steady practice today reflects who I am becoming, not just how I wish to be seen??

Day 339

My legacy is shaped by how I handle hard moments.

INSIGHT

People remember how you showed up when things got tough. The tone, the care, the steadiness, that's what lasts.

REFLECTION QUESTION

How am I shaping trust during challenges?

Day 340

I mentor others by showing what growth looks like.

INSIGHT

Mentoring isn't about giving answers; it's about living the questions alongside someone else. Your example becomes their encouragement.

REFLECTION QUESTION

What part of my own growth journey could help someone else?

Day 341

My mentorship builds a future beyond me.

INSIGHT

Your leadership doesn't end with your role. Mentorship is how your values and lessons continue, even when you step aside.

REFLECTION QUESTION

Who am I mentoring now, and what values am I passing on through that relationship?

Day 342

I lead by modeling what matters, not by demanding it.

INSIGHT

You can't build trust by instruction alone. People observe your tone, boundaries, and consistency. What you do teaches louder than what you say.

REFLECTION QUESTION

What am I teaching others just by how I show up?

Day 343

I prepare successors with humility, not control, so they can lead in ways I never could.

INSIGHT

Leadership isn't about replication - it's about helping others rise in their own way. Grow impact, not ego.

REFLECTION QUESTION

How am I helping someone lead with confidence, not conformity?

I honor those who came before me by leading with care.

INSIGHT

You're not the first, and you won't be the last. Leadership is a continuum. Lead as if someone will inherit what you build, because they will.

REFLECTION QUESTION

What leadership habit am I leaving behind for someone else?

Day 345

I lead beyond ego.

INSIGHT

Legacy isn't about being remembered, it's about making a difference. The more you release control, the more others rise.

REFLECTION QUESTION

Where could letting go increase my impact?

Day 346

*I lead with care,
knowing even quiet
ripples can outlast my
presence.*

INSIGHT

Leadership isn't measured in recognition—it's felt in the culture you shape and the tone you set. Those quiet ripples live on in others.

REFLECTION QUESTION

What quiet tone or habit am I setting that might ripple forward?

Day 347

I prepare others to lead with strength I may never witness.

INSIGHT

Legacy isn't about being followed, it's about making space for others to lead. Nurture leaders, not dependence, and your impact will outlast your presence. True leadership lets go.

REFLECTION QUESTION

Whose leadership am I quietly shaping by stepping aside?

Day 348

I trust that my daily leadership is building a legacy of subtle impact.

INSIGHT

Not all influence is visible at once. The ripple effect of consistent, values-driven actions accumulates quietly over time.

REFLECTION QUESTION

How do my actions today reflect the legacy I wish to leave behind?

Day 349

I define my success by the positive impact I create, not by temporary wins.

INSIGHT

True success lies in the lasting influence of my actions—how they inspire and elevate others over time.

REFLECTION QUESTION

What impact today will resonate in the days to come?

Day 350

I step forward confidently, knowing impact is measured by the lives I touch.

INSIGHT

My legacy is built on consistent, values-driven decisions that create ripples long after the moment has passed.

REFLECTION QUESTION

What small act today contributes to the legacy I hope to leave behind?

Day 351

My impact is measured in people, not popularity.

INSIGHT

Legacy isn't built on applause. It's built on trust, growth, and the lives you've helped shape along the way.

REFLECTION QUESTION

Who is better because I've led with care?

Day 352

Legacy is not what you achieve, it's how you treat people along the way.

INSIGHT

People may forget your strategy, but they'll remember how you made them feel. Kindness leaves a longer trail than control.

REFLECTION QUESTION

How does the way I lead today reflect what matters most about my character?

Day 353

I leave a legacy defined by thoughtful actions, not fleeting moments.

INSIGHT

Legacy isn't built on accolades. It's shaped by the lasting influence of your daily choices, grounded in care, consistency, and purpose.

REFLECTION QUESTION

What small act today will shape how I'm remembered tomorrow?

Day 354

I prepare others for leadership through consistent mentorship.

INSIGHT

By nurturing potential in others, you extend your influence beyond your own tenure. True leadership is multiplied in the success of those you mentor.

REFLECTION QUESTION

Who can I invest in today to help cultivate future leaders?

Day 355

Sometimes the hardest call is the most human one.

INSIGHT

Not every decision will please everyone. But choosing the path that honors dignity—even at a cost—is often the bravest.

REFLECTION QUESTION

What human-centered choice am I willing to stand by?

Day 356

I prepare my legacy by nurturing my growth and the growth of those around me.

INSIGHT

Building for the future means investing in both your own evolution and that of others.

REFLECTION QUESTION

What step can I take today to empower future leaders?

I leave a legacy defined by thoughtful action and heartfelt service.

INSIGHT

My impact is measured not by fleeting moments, but by the consistent care and intentionality I bring to every interaction.

REFLECTION QUESTION

What thoughtful act today will echo in my legacy tomorrow?

Day 358

Every decision I make molds the legacy I leave behind.

INSIGHT

My daily choices are the brushstrokes of my long-term impact. Focusing on what truly matters ensures that I build a legacy of purpose and integrity.

REFLECTION QUESTION

What decision today will I look back on as foundational to my legacy?

Day 359

I live my purpose with quiet consistency.

INSIGHT

Purpose doesn't need to be loud to be lasting. When you live with steady intention and quiet care, your daily actions become part of something enduring, something greater than yourself.

REFLECTION QUESTION

How can I let today's small act reflect the deeper purpose I carry?

Day 360

*My greatest impact
may not be immediate.*

INSIGHT

Legacy often unfolds in hindsight. Don't underestimate the quiet influence you carry through consistency and care.

REFLECTION QUESTION

What quiet influence am I offering today?

Day 361

I build legacy by creating space for others to co-own the mission.

INSIGHT

Legacy isn't just what you finish, it's what you build together. When others share ownership, the mission lasts beyond you. A true legacy is carried forward by the team, not just remembered by them.

REFLECTION QUESTION

Where can I release control to make space for co-creation?

Day 362

Legacy is built in the unseen structure of daily leadership.

INSIGHT

Systems don't just move tasks—they carry your vision. Build them with care. When the process aligns with your values, your legacy stays strong.

REFLECTION QUESTION

What process am I reinforcing—and does it reflect what matters most?

Day 363

I hold the vision for the future in both mind and heart.

INSIGHT

When your aspirations align with your actions, you create a steady path toward lasting impact.

REFLECTION QUESTION

What future reality am I committed to building?

Day 364

I plant trees whose shade I may never sit under.

INSIGHT

Some of your most meaningful contributions will benefit people you'll never meet. That doesn't diminish your impact—it deepens it.

REFLECTION QUESTION

What long-term investment am I making today, even if the reward comes later?

Part 10

The Return

"Leadership begins again."

Day 365

I pause with gratitude, then return to the work ahead with renewed clarity, courage, and a sense of contribution.

INSIGHT

Leadership doesn't end—it deepens. In the space between this day and the next, take time to pause. This quiet moment isn't a break from leadership—it's part of it.

You've done more than complete a practice. You've cultivated presence, strengthened purpose, and prepared to return—not just to work, but to the kind of leader you choose to be.

REFLECTION QUESTIONS

This last moment offers more than a single prompt. These questions are meant to stay with you—guiding your next challenge, your next conversation, your next quiet act of leadership. Return to them whenever you need direction.

1. What daily practices will help me carry this work forward with purpose and presence?
2. Where have I already seen signs that my leadership has made a difference?
3. How can I lead with values when pressure, distraction, or doubt show up again?
4. What will remind me to return—to reflection, to clarity, to growth—when I need it most?

CLOSING THOUGHTS

Pause here. Not to mark an ending, but to recognize how far you've come.

What feels clearer now than when you began? What habits are taking root? What kind of leader are you becoming—by intention, not by default?

The affirmations weren't the destination. They were tools to surface your values, question your assumptions, and steady your presence. What matters most is what you carry forward: into your next conversation, your next decision, your next challenge.

Leadership isn't something you earn once. It's a daily practice. It shows in how you handle pressure, build trust, and respond when it would be easier to stay quiet.

This isn't a finish line. It's a continuation.

Lead from that deeper place. Keep going.

Free Companion Download

The Presence Practice: A Daily or Weekly Practice for Reflective Leadership

This companion resource offers a simple, five-step reflective practice inspired by contemplative traditions and designed for modern leaders. It helps you pause, realign with your values, and lead with clarity, courage, and contribution.

Use it as a quiet daily ritual or a weekly pause to ground your leadership in what matters most.

Download your free copy here:

383

About the Author

Dr. Dan H. Lawrence is an educator, strategist, and lifelong learner with three decades of experience spanning libraries, nonprofits, higher education, and the public sector. His nonfiction works center on helping leaders navigate uncertainty with clarity, act with courage, and contribute meaningfully to the communities they serve.

With a background in educational leadership, instructional design, and information science, Dan brings a grounded and thoughtful approach to leadership and organizational change. Values of service, reflection, and discernment shape his career

Through his writing, Dan invites others to pause, realign with their values, and lead with purpose even in the most challenging times.